Anchored
to the Son

Pursuing Christ when the Storm Calms

Adam Holland

To all souls burdened by storms and troubles, come calm and quiet your soul in Jesus Christ where true and abiding rest, recovery, and hope can be found. As Jesus says in Matthew 11:28-30, "Come to me, all who labor and are heavy laden, and I will give you rest. Take my yoke upon you, and learn from me, for I am gentle and lowly in heart, and you will find rest for your souls. For my yoke is easy and my burden is light."

Contents

To the Reader

Four years* to the day since I first heard the word "cancer," I sat in my living room and penned these first words for *Anchored to the Son: Pursuing Christ when the Storm Calms*. Over these past years, the crises rose and fell into a pleasant calm; my prayers have changed over these four years from praying for my own health to praying for you and the trials, sufferings, and storms you face, and praying each day for the readers of *Anchored in the Storm*. The idea and concept of "recovery" is a regular thought of mine, but seems a bit off, even as I near five years of a cancer-free life.

As an aside, I have to say that over the years since *Anchored in the Storm* was released, the Lord has filled my heart with joy and care for you. I have absolutely loved praying for the book's readers every single day. Seeing reader's lives changed to greater understanding, growth, and strength in Christ has been an absolute privilege. The Lord always surprises me, and His answers to prayers are always beyond what one would expect and always for our good. *Anchored in the Storm* was for you and the subtitle says it all: *Pursuing Christ in the Midst of Life's Trials*. At the end of the day, Christ must be everything, in the storm and in the calm.

Christians and the church often talk of suffering as a part of the Christian life. Jesus says himself in John 16:33: "I have said these things to you, that in me you may have peace. *In the world you will have tribulation.* But take heart; I have overcome the world" (emphasis mine). In this world, in this life outside of the presence of God in Heaven we, as Christians, can expect suffering. In some ways, it is a part of our Christian DNA on this earth.

Suffering is a guarantee, Christ-follower, and so is healing when the suffering subsides. But I think healing is a much more subtle, slow transition from suffering back to a "normal" life than not. However, we realize that we ourselves have changed and our way of life before the trial is gone. What does the Bible say about recovery, after the suffering has passed and we return to an "ordinary" life? (As I have become accustomed to saying a "new normal" life.) I can only pray that *Anchored to the Son: Pursuing Christ when the Storm Calms* is an adequate answer to the question: "what do I do when the trial ends?"

Since my diagnosis, treatment, and end of the physical part of my cancer trial, thoughts of recovery have swirled around in my mind. Thoughts of what the word means, how the Lord works in these times after a trial, and what the Lord desires from this return to normality. As I thought, and continue to think about recovery, I often go back to the first ideas and words I wrote when the thoughts of *Anchored to the Son* was just begging to get out on paper. I thought of the beach. Time after time this visual of the sand, waves, and ocean breeze cemented itself upon my mind. I can still envision it now as I write as I first did years ago.

Here you stand on the same beach I stood upon when my storm calmed. You blink your eyes a few times as if you had just awakened; you look around realizing you are standing on the beach, bruised, and battered. You look around quizzically, trying to make sense of your surroundings. Yet, as you awaken and look around, you see everyone else on the beach enjoying a bright, warm day, having fun, laughing, living it up as if there was not a storm anywhere in sight. Life for them was not challenged or afflicted, it continued on carefree. Most on the beach were unaffected or unaware of any storm, particularly your storm, and frankly, most probably do not realize you are there standing, hurting, bruised, and battered, but gratefully alive. But there you stand looking out into the crisp waters where miles out you suffered in the storm with waves and winds coursing around you. Some may question your battered appearance. Some may be interested in your story, but most on the beach are interested in a day at the beach over your return to the calm of life after the storm. For the most part, this new journey of recovery is down to you and Jesus together again to face a different part of life, coming out of a trial to return to a different life you never anticipated.

You were wondering while out at sea if you would survive, and if you did survive what life would look like when it is all over. As you stand on the warm sand feeling the cool breeze on you, you take a deep breath of that fresh beach air contemplating life ahead, and you realize and recognize that most of the old life is gone. The ease, comfort, and peace of life before the storm have vanished. The road ahead may be just as hard as the storm was. It may be just as long, if not longer, than the suffering. The toll on your soul seems unimaginable to contemplate, but your life as a Christ-follower is forcing you to continue the journey in a new direction, down a new road, into a "new normal."

Here you and I stand, survivors of a great storm, eager to get on with our lives, but struggling to do so. As I thought about standing on that beach, I looked around for something that would help the transition into the "new normal" of my life, a phrase I have used more times than I can count. I am sure there is something great out there, but I was not immediately aware of it and realized that part of my own recovery from brain cancer may take writing this book. I was an amateur when I got cancer and I am an amateur in my recovery, but I am eager to write a book that will help many of those who have been blessed by the first book. This is much more about you than me, much more about Christ than us. It was a great joy to write *Anchored in the Storm*; it is another great joy to write *Anchored to the Son*. Know that as you were desperately prayed for in your storm, that I again desperately pray the Lord's hand upon you in recovery and that these two books might change lives and bring Christ to the forefront of our suffering and now recovery.

On my bathroom mirror at home and taped to my computer in my classroom is a saying, "There is much to be done. Let's not lose sight." The Lord has chosen you to survive this trial for a purpose. His purpose for me in surviving was to write these two *Anchored* books, a thought I still cannot wrap my mind around. The Lord has used the books in ways I cannot fathom. And whether you write a book, talk with a friend, take on a new perspective, or bold attitude in Christ, there is much to be done for His kingdom. You and I survived our storm because the Lord has more for us to do. He does not need us to do His work, but He does want to partner with us for His work.

One example of not losing sight and seeing this world with the Lord's perspective and continuing Christ's work is my dear friend and sister in Christ from Kansas, Allie Montgomery. Allie was diagnosed with the same cancer, in almost the same spot in the brain, as I was. Though in Kansas, we connected through the CERN Foundation, and Allie, her husband Mitch, and parents Chris and Doneen Childress, all became family to me. It was Christ and the cancer that brought us together during the summer of 2019. We met in Dallas while I went to visit my friends, Steve and Lesly Stark. Cancer has a way of tearing our souls apart, but Christ gave us a great gift in bringing us all together. Our mended souls all met and relished our time together praising and honoring the Lord through His work in our lives and storms. Allie and her family are fighting to raise money for Ependymoma, the cancer both Allie and I had, with Christlike passion and love for those afflicted by this incredibly rare brain cancer.

The purpose for you is unique to the Lord's calling on your life. Surviving means the day is not done and there is more to your story and impact in Christ on this earth. He is still building His kingdom and He wants you to be a part of building the kingdom alongside Him! Let us journey this road to recovery together seeking the Lord, His will over our lives, and His kingdom. "There is much to be done. Let's not lose sight."

What if "recovery," as we think of it as restoration of the way things were before the storm, is not what the Lord has called us to? What if the Lord has called us to a *renewed* life instead of a *recovered* life? The shadow of cancer and its possible return still hangs over me. I know that shadow of cancer will be a companion, but is no longer a worrisome companion. I have to accept the very real possibility of its return. However, I have a greater companion than the shadow of cancer I'm closer to, and His name is Jesus Christ. He knows my past, my present, and my future and even with my imperfect life still loves me, and chooses to work wonders in my life on a daily basis. I can only pray that I would embrace the Lord's work once again knowing that He will work just as faithfully and graciously as He did before.

Think for a moment about Jesus coming from Heaven down into our world. He had to take everything He knew and become human. Jesus had never been human and though He created us, didn't know what it was like. He had to learn to walk just as we learned to walk. The same goes for speaking, eating, working, reading, and all the other skills that are essential to humanity. He had to learn these things as you and I have to learn to heal, to recover, to start life again with new knowledge and skills we take from our journey through the storm.

And as we talk about healing, we need to remember that Christ teaches us about life after the storm, a life of calm, restful trust and resiliency in Him. You can trust Him because He walked the same exact road you have in this life, but without sin: the same exact life, trials, and all. No god of any other religion has walked the same footsteps of creation, the footsteps you are presently walking, with the desire to save and heal you. Only Christ has those qualifications and with Him we can be restored to the original creation He intended life to be for us.

As we start this new journey of *Anchored to the Son*, know that this book is really just a book of a changed life. A changed life by the presence and handiwork of God Almighty. Peace be to you dear brother and dear sister as we go forth to live our "new normal" seeking Christ above all things.

In your Christian life, I pray you will find that one life touches another and that we truly do not walk this life alone. Two people out of so very many whom I've had the great pleasure to walk this life with present brief, but poignant, forewords to *Anchored to the Son*. The first is Dr. R.W. Mackey. I've had the immense joy of knowing R.W. most of my life, growing up with his kids, sitting under his spiritual and professional teaching at church and at The Master's University. He brings a brief foreword of the Lord's work in his own trial of a harrowing cycling accident and his thoughts as he and his wife, Beth, start their "new normal."

The second foreword is from my pastor, Todd Smith. Todd was such a presence in my storm that I could not write this book without a few poignant words from him. He has had his own storms in life, and through his journey as pastor of Crossroads Community Church, has had to learn from the storms and move on towards God's calling upon us for the sake of His cause.

To the Reader was begun in 2018 on the fourth anniversary of having brain surgery to remove the cancer in 2014. *Anchored to the Son* was finished in the summer of 2019, five years after this surgery, and published in 2021.

Foreword

R.W. Mackey

The Master's University Professor
Crossroads Community Church Elder

Just because it's a cliché, doesn't mean it's untrue...so it is with the saying, "life can turn on a dime." My life did.

Not only was I married to the dearest woman on earth, but my life's rhythm held great joy for me. Teaching university courses in Business and Economics to young Christ-followers, serving as an elder for our vibrant church, watching our four children, with their spouses, parent our eleven grandchildren; and feeling the exhilaration of riding a bicycle competitively seemed like the perfect life's script for a man moving into his "golden years!" This all changed in an instant! I would tell you exactly what happened, but I don't know. In one second, I'm returning from a long, hard training ride. Twenty-four hours later, I began brief, intermittent moments of lucidity which dotted the next three weeks – a large portion of which was spent in Intensive Care. My riding buddy (a dear friend and colleague) thought I was dying after I crashed head-first into a post. The surgeon who initially kept me alive (and has been putting me back together for the past 2 years) told my wife, "He may not make it," before performing an emergency tracheotomy and blood transfusion. I had gone from being a top-form, endurance senior athlete to sustaining a brain bleed, a broken neck, broken jaw, a face separated from my thrice-fractured skull, a shattered nose, and a fractured shoulder blade. A myriad number of other cuts, bruises, and sprains riddled the rest of me. Even my sight was pretty much gone.

As my strength and coherence increased, the Father's work in my heart accompanied. He began...

- allowing me to sense His presence in His time and His way.

- softening my heart toward hurting people.

- teaching me that my times are in His hands; He is in absolute control.

- showing me the value of serving people.

- taking greater vestiges of pride from me.

- showing me the precious worth of the woman who so graciously transitioned from "for better" to "for worse."

Fourteen doctors, five surgeries, and three dentists later; my life would still be best described by another cliché: a "new normal." In fact, I will carry constant reminders to my grave...Reminders of what? That I live in a fallen world where gut-wrenching things happen to all sorts of people. That brief moments can leave lasting results. That I experienced a "crash" (not an accident) because nothing happens by accident to a child of God. That untested faith may not be faith at all. That God is real and near. That I may never know why things happen (God doesn't owe me an explanation). That God's people really do emanate His love. That Romans 8:28 is true! That I hope the fires of trial allow me to "come forth as gold" (Job 23:10, NASB).

Truth is, my crash and the possibility of more hardship were not and are not on my wish-list! Yet, I wouldn't trade the work of God in my heart born from my experience. As I launch into my earthly life after the crash, I'm learning to move on while maintaining the warmth of His presence discovered in my infirmity. I don't want to live in the past, but I want the past to deeply affect me. I want to keep my Lord centrally in focus the way He was in the darkest hour.

I know Adam's desire in composing his first book and now, although it seems paradoxical, this one is to remain anchored when the sailing resumes!

Foreword

Pastor Todd Smith

Crossroads Community Church

In the Spring of 2012 God made me lie down. He had asked me to lie down many times before this Spring, but I was too busy doing things for Him. The green pasture he picked was a hospital bed. This turned into a yearlong pause on my life. The good shepherd knew what I needed, and it turned out to be the best days of my life. In fact, it saved my life. You see, I thought I was in control of my life and I could shepherd myself. Well, that is a lie from the pit. This lie can so easily destroy you and those that you love.

Sometimes God uses storms of life to remind us that we are not in control, but He is in control. Storms make us lie down. For me, the storm was a green pasture. It is at those moments of time we have choices to make. Either we can fight with the Lord and curse the storm, or we can trust the Lord and embrace the storm. Embrace all that God has to teach us during those dark nights of the soul. Over the decades I have learned that a warm embrace of the sovereign plan of God for my life is the only way to go. Fighting Him is a losing battle. God has a baseball card and it says a billion wins and zero losses.

The crazy storms of this life are times of surrender and times to lie down next to the Good Shepherd. This life can really kick your teeth and we must learn to surrender to His sovereignty and to trust it. Trust that He not only knows but he also cares very deeply. The great promise of the Good Shepherd is that He is with us. The shepherd is never closer than in the chaos of the storm. The chaos of the storm is not because He is absent. He is right there.

We must stop and lie down in His sovereign grace and ride out the storm. Fighting Him is futile but fighting for faith and trust is essential.

Once again, Adam Holland leads the reader not just through the storm but out of the storm. He reminds us that our dependence on Him is not lessened once the storm ends but as needed as ever. Don't be fooled into thinking that our dependence on Christ is only needed in the storms of life. We must anchor ourselves in the quiet moments of life. We must lie down in the pasture regularly to gain the needed rest for the next storm or even momentary rough waters. Our shepherd is not just with us in the dark days, He is with us in the sunny moments of life.

Adam tells a story of trust and faith that we can all relate to. In his intimate style, he takes you to the deep moments of life where Jesus is so present and so real. He creates a thirst in each of us to seek and desire a walk with Jesus that is real, meaningful and restful. Sit and soak in the words of this book as you walk out of your storms and follow your Shepherd. God has green pastures ahead, and this book will help you find those places.

Pastor Todd W. Smith

1

Groanings
for the New Life

"So we are always of good courage. We know that while we are at home in the body we are away from the Lord, for we walk by faith, not by sight. We are of good courage, and we would rather be away from the body and at home with the Lord. So whether we are at home or away, we make it our aim to please him."

~ 2 Corinthians 5:6-9

———◆———

During the difficult times, have you ever groaned, "How long, O Lord?" Wondering when the trial would end, how much longer will you have to endure? How much longer until it is over and you can get back to living life again? David writes an entire psalm in Psalm 13, on this one question, particularly on how long will it be until the Lord acts. Have you ever asked that question when life was good, and the days were bright? I know I never had before the storm. Now though, I have asked this, "How long, O Lord, can the chaos of our 21st century world continue? How long before you return, O Lord?"

"How long, O Lord?" is a question that has been asked for thousands of years from David to the Corinthians to you and I. Paul addresses the question in 2 Corinthians 5:1-10. Take a moment to read those 10 verses. The Corinthians are wondering about the imminent return of Christ as they see the world collapsing around them: the hostility of Christians throughout the Roman Empire, the tyranny of the Roman government over the known world, the promise from Christ Himself of His return, which they thought would be during their lifetimes. Their groanings of the situation are the same groanings and sighs we have today in an increasingly hostile world, a world turned against Christ and His followers. If we are not groaning regarding our own situation, I am sure we have groaned over the chaos and uncertainties of the world.

Paul understands the anxieties faced by the church at Corinth and their desire for a different world, a world completely and absolutely under the control of the Lord. He knows the eagerness of the Corinthian readers because he has the same eagerness to see the present world pass. Paul refers to this present world as a tent. Since I am not really a camper, I am not overly familiar with tents. I do know they are temporary structures, somewhat open to the elements, not meant to be the most comfortable, used during a journey, and after any type of use will break down in time. This world is a mere tent, but if I am honest and if you are honest, we do not really see this world as temporary. We see this world as home. Home is permanent, or at least that is how we think and live. We build and furnish our homes, our monuments to ourselves, as if we expect to be here forever. But there is a small part of us that longs for something more, a reality beyond this one.

Solomon, David's son, knows how it feels to be a part of this world and yet to long for eternity. Ecclesiastes 3:11 says, "He has made everything beautiful in its time. Also, he has put eternity into man's hearts, yet so that he cannot find out what God has done from the beginning to end." Our earthly presence is passing, and Paul writes in 2 Corinthians 5:1, "For we know that if the tent that is our earthly home is destroyed, we have a building from God, a house not made with hands, eternal in the heavens." Did you notice it? It's not a tent anymore, but "a building from God."

This world is all we know and sometimes we presume that life will continue on here forever; we know nothing else. Sometimes we also feel that our suffering will continue on or will at some point return. It can be hard to look ahead, and it can be hard to look at the here and now. It is as if our hearts are torn between worlds, but deep down we know we long for Heaven. And our heart groans because we are still here on earth.

As hard as it is to live here, Paul reminds us of the great guarantee we have in Christ, to be with Him in Heaven, forever. He encourages us in 2 Corinthians 5:5 that "He who has prepared us for this very thing is God, who has given us the Spirit as a guarantee." In this time where we are struggling to build our tents here and awaiting His kingdom to come, through God's presence we are assured of our future. We are assured of our permanent home in Heaven, not the temporary tent, but a permanent palace.

There were times when I was going through the uncertain chaos of cancer, not knowing how many days, months, or years I had ahead, that I truly thought the Lord would take my life to Heaven sooner than later. This is going to sound odd, but there were times I had hoped that I was in the final count of my days left on this earth. It is strange to think that I was longing for death, but on the other hand, it felt so very natural. Deep down I knew, and continue to know, this is not home. My longing is to be in Christ's presence, to have this world pass away.

The Lord has reminded me time and time again that there is great purpose of His children to remain on this earth, to minister to believers, to share the gospel with unbelievers, and to live entirely for Him, a shining light to our increasingly dark and darkening world. The Lord has reminded me time after time, "So whether we are at home or away, we make it our aim to please him" (2 Corinthians 5:9).

2

Restore, Confirm, Strengthen, Establish

"And after you have suffered a little while, the God of all grace, who has called you to his eternal glory in Christ, will himself restore, confirm, strengthen and establish you."

~ 1 Peter 5:10

———————— ◆ ————————

God is going to work in our lives as God is going to work in our lives. He does what He does many times without us understanding why He works in certain ways. We know that God has His own timetable, not ours, and certainly not ours when we are suffering. Peter writes about God's timing in 2 Peter 3:8: "But do not overlook this one fact, beloved, that with the Lord one day is as a thousand years, and a thousand years as one day." He is not burdened by time, as you and I are, so it is not too much for Him to wait 1,000 years for something to happen or for His will to be done. He knows He is going to act, and it is His prerogative to act when He wants, in the ways He wants, at the time He wants.

As God has timed the universe according to His clock, so He has also timed your suffering to His clock. Peter writes in his first book, "After you have suffered a little while." I know you are looking back on your trials and thinking, "But God, that was years of torment, how was this short?" Remember though, 2 Peter 3:8 above and also remember that Job says in Job 7:7, "Remember that my life is a breath." In God's timetable, a human life is like a breath, a mere vapor here for a second, gone a second later. Those decades we have spent building lives and relationships on this earth are practically nothing in the timetable of the Lord. And the wonderful thing is that the Lord's got it all under control. One thousand years and 1,000 days are the same to Him. God will spend what seems like 1,000 years in one day of your life. He isn't looking at the time spent, He is looking at the process.

God will spend the time He needs in your life to bring you to a certain place through suffering, but in every way, this side of Heaven or in Heaven with Him, He will bring your suffering to an end. Peter writes that God, with His unending grace, is going to restore, confirm, strengthen, and establish each of us. Let us take a short look at each of those promises and see God's role in bringing calm back to our lives.

Restore

When we hear the word "suffer" we probably think of Job, and to a certain extent that is a good thing because God has shown us so much through Job's suffering.

Job's suffering cost him everything: all his livestock, servants, property, health, and most precious to him, his children. An extremely wealthy man at the opening, Job comes to utter destitution just one chapter into the book. At the end of the book the author writes in Job 42:10, "And the Lord restored the fortunes of Job … the Lord gave Job twice as much as he had before," including seven sons and three daughters. Everything and more was restored to Job.

For those of us who have suffered, was our experience like that? Did you get back everything you lost two-fold? Many times, the things we lost during our trials stay lost. God is working in your life differently than He did in Job's life. So, what does it mean that God is going to "restore" or "perfect"? To be made more like Christ, so you look and act more like Christ than yourself, with a deeper and more significant life.

Remember that our suffering has been about one thing, Jesus Christ, that we may be refined to be more like Him, to grow closer to Him. God may restore all your physical fortunes, comforts, and health. But even more important is the restored, strengthened, intimate, perfected relationship you have with Christ.

Confirm

In our suffering, God was trying to take our eyes off of ourselves and off of this world, to turn them on Him. He is not testing your salvation. If you are in Christ, you are forever in Christ, but He is testing the depth of your heart. It is as if He is asking you, how much are you in this, the family of God? How much like Christ are you? He wants all of you and this is an opportunity for you and the Lord to pray over how much of your life He has and for Him to show you areas that you can work on while you recover and return to a life unburdened of your suffering. At the end of your suffering He wants to hear you say, "I'm in!" no matter what.

Peter uses "confirm" again in 2 Peter 1:3-9 where he talks about what God has given us through His divine power. He gives us characteristics we can work on during any time of our lives, but even more so as we exit the storm and start to rebuild life. Peter talks about virtue, knowledge, self-control, steadfastness, godliness, brotherly affection, and finally love. We are not going to master these qualities alone, but only through a strong relationship with Christ. What better time to start focusing and implementing these qualities while we are starting again in this life with the help of the Spirit, the storm behind us, the Son ahead.

Strengthen

Our trials, whether physical or emotional, take their toll on our strengths. When I finished my radiation treatments and chemotherapy, there was great joy in my life, but I was weak and exhausted and would be for months on end for the next year. God promised to strengthen us and as we have discussed, not all the strength is physical, and even more so it should be spiritual.

There are two ways the Lord strengthens us. The first is by His hand. Isaiah says, "Strengthen the weak hands, and make firm the feeble knees" (Isaiah 35:3). The Lord is going to provide the strength through His grace to rise each morning, face the day, and walk in the Spirit throughout the day. He is strengthening you for His work and His glory. He wants you to take what you have learned in your suffering and share it with a world in need of Christ's salvation. We are not called to learn something and hold onto it as if it was just for us. We are called to share what Christ has done.

The second way the Lord strengthens us is inspiring us to grow all on our own, to take what we have learned and expand on our experiences and knowledge. The author of Hebrews writes in Hebrews 12:12-13, "Therefore, lift your drooping hands and strengthen your weak knees, and make straight paths for your feet so that what is lame may not be put out of joint but rather be healed." Our lives as Christ-followers are not to be passive, sitting there on the couch doing nothing, but they are meant to be active and alive, useful and purposeful in all things for Christ. God is active in your life, but in His wisdom, He wants us to work also at our faith, for His kingdom. As He has provided healing, so He is asking you to do what you can for the sake of your own being, and even greater, your relationship with Him. The reality is of course that we can't do it on our own and need Christ, but many times God gives us the tools and responsibilities to share the gospel and to expand the kingdom.

Establish

Since the dawn of time, God wanted a relationship with His creation. However, in our great pursuit of this world and our own desires, over pursuing God, we pushed Him aside, out of our lives. Since the fall of humanity and the disruption of relationship, He has worked to establish and restore our relationship with Him. He was executed on the cross for your sake, that the relationship between God and mankind would be restored. He chose to take the initiative on reestablishing a relationship with us. He reached out to you with a call to salvation. He calls and we respond.

After the storm has passed, He is asking you to reflect on what you have been through and what you have learned. What does life look like for you in the calm from the storm? What does your relationship with Him look like? Dwell on 2 Corinthians 1:21-22 for a few minutes: "And it is God who establishes us with you in Christ, and has anointed us, and who has also put his seal on us and given us his Spirit in our hearts as a guarantee."

In all trials, the Lord wants to know that He is the primary person in our relationship. He created you, died for you, reached out to you with salvation, and wants to grow in relationship with you. He wants you and loves you. In this life, we need a variety of reminders throughout our walk of faith of the privilege we have of being part of His family. We are chosen for Him, of no significance of our own, but for His will, good pleasure, and glory.

At the end of these four promises that God gives us after suffering, to whom do they belong? To a certain extent yes, you are restored, confirmed, strengthened, and established, but ultimately, as with all things, they belong to the Lord. The suffering and restoration are all His, by His time, for His glory. You get to play an incredible role in being restored, confirmed, strengthened, and established in Him. The Lord has set you up for a great future, closer to Him than before, willing to work as He wills for the spread of the gospel and the expansion of His kingdom, and at the end of the day, it's all for Him and His glory.

Pray over those four promises and acts of the Lord and go forth in faith in Christ.

3

Stay Awake

"But concerning that day or that hour, no one knows, not even the angels in heaven, nor the Son, but only the Father. Be on guard, keep awake. For you do not know when the time will come. It is like a man going on a journey, when he leaves home and puts his servants in charge, each with his work and commands the doorkeeper to stay awake. Therefore, stay awake – for you do not know when the master of the house will come, in the evening or at midnight, or when the rooster crows, or in the morning – lest he come suddenly and find you asleep. And what I say to you I say to all: 'Stay Awake.'"

~ Mark 13:32-37

There are days throughout our lives that will always stand out to us, days and moments that are forever embedded in our memories. They could be newsworthy days such as the Apollo moon landing, the fall of the Soviet Union, the 9/11 attacks, coronavirus. They could be personal memories such as a wedding, birth of a child, or a life-changing conversation.

A day is coming that will be so embedded in our minds that no one alive will ever forget. That day is the return of Jesus Christ to earth. There is only One who knows the exact day, the exact hour, the exact moment Jesus will come back to earth, God the Father. Mark writes earlier in Mark 12:26: "And then they will see the Son of Man coming in clouds with great power and glory." On this exact day, the world will turn to the skies and see something this world has never seen, Jesus Christ returning to earth. Assuredly, the day is coming!

Jesus is telling His disciples and future followers, you and me, to "Stay Awake," be prepared, be on the lookout, do not get caught up with the trappings of this world should you be so occupied with life that you miss it. This world is all we know, the people and places. This world is home, or at least we say it is home. We are comfortable here and we spend most of our time here making our lives as comfortable as we can, especially in prosperous America. As we make this life ours, we tune out what Christ is saying. Christ says, "Stay Alert!" while our heart says, "I'm busy! I've got things to do! Jesus, hang on while I do _____ (fill in the blank)." We distract ourselves with entertainment, careers, sports, family, marriage, things that matter to us on this earth. But these things are not overly important in the kingdom of the Lord. He is of utmost importance and should have the supreme place in our lives, all parts of our lives.

The Lord is asking us, in a way, to act as children do when something important is going to happen. I remember several occasions when my grandparents came for a visit and I just couldn't wait to see them. The day before I could hardly sleep, thinking about what we were going to do, what they will say, and as any kid would ask, "Will they bring me anything?" In the morning and throughout the day I would not have a clue as to when they were going to arrive, but I knew it was today. My parents would be busy preparing food, cleaning the house, and I would help always looking out the front window to see if they had arrived. And then in the midst of the busyness of preparing for the visit, the doorbell would ring. They were here!

With that same enthusiasm and excitement, we should anticipate the return of Christ. In this one moment the entirety of history, life, everything we know has shifted: some for good, some for bad. But he is coming back!

Are we like a child, eagerly awaiting the Lord's return? Are we staying awake? Are we ready for the return of Christ? If I'm honest with myself, I'm not 100% sure if I'm ready. There are things I would still like to do, places I would like to visit, and a few things in my heart I need to take care of. If we are honest, we are not ready. But Christ is calling us to "Stay Awake!" and be ready.

If your trial is fading or is over now, it is the perfect time to consider your present life in this world and whether or not you are ready for Christ's return. He is not calling us to build homes here, but Christ is asking us to be ready, alert, and awake! The way this world is presently heading, it is easy to say that Christ's return is soon, but God may tarry through even darker times on this earth and we may have to endure more difficult trials before His return.

In this moment, are you presently ready, alert, and awake for His return? He's coming!

4

By Faith, Not Sight

"So we are always of good courage. We know that while we are at home in the body we are away from the Lord, for we walk by faith, not by sight."

~ Mark 13:32-37

———— ♦ ————

What I am going to say right now is not something I have often told people over the years since I was diagnosed with cancer. In 2015 I was declared cancer-free, but in my mind, I knew it would come back, and would come back with a vengeance. Each small headache, each moment when I felt a little off, I knew then the cancer had returned. And I anticipated the scan that confirmed it and confirmed a final prognosis and of how much time I had left to live.

In many ways, I was certain this would happen. I remember for a time I had prayed the Lord would take me in my sleep. It was nothing morbid or dark; I felt as if I had done what the Lord had wanted me to do during the cancer and in writing *Anchored in the Storm*. I was eager to move on into a life in the presence of Christ that was far better than the best day I ever had in this life on earth. I regularly thought about 2 Corinthians 5:8: "Yes, we are of good courage, and we would rather be away from the body and at home with the Lord." I longed and longed and longed for this just as Paul did.

However, each brain scan up to present has come back clear. Few minor changes here and there, but no cancer. I realized that I was facing life ahead and I have to learn to live that life post-cancer. My days are still numbered, as are yours, and while I thought I had fewer days ahead, I actually had many more. Before, during, and after the cancer, I faced a life, in many ways, I hadn't expected. Now it was time to think about a life I hadn't intended, a life beyond the cancer, a life where I had years and decades left, a career fulfilled, possibly even retirement. It does not necessarily scare me, but it is not what I had anticipated and have to consider a life ahead I had never really thought about.

As I have recovered and the scans came back clear, the Lord and I have had many conversations and dialogues regarding what my life is to be like. In some ways I had argued with the Lord, "I'm not supposed to be here, I'm supposed to be with You!" Paul in 2 Corinthians explained it all, explained my very heart there on the pages of the Bible. My heart longed to be with Christ, to live in a world completely under His generous and gracious care, a world and a life in Christ, without the burden and effects of sin around me. The desire is still there, but the reality is I am here in this world and in this life.

The reality of the life I presently face came before verse 8 in verses 6-7: "So we are always of good courage. We know that while we are at home in the body we are away from the Lord, for we walk by faith, not by sight." It is a stark reality of being away from the Lord, having been so intimately connected during the storm, and yet for this time of life, we are away from the Lord. In some ways living in this world is its own storm, its own trial, a life where calm is not known. Even what we call "calm" is not a calm like that in the presence of the Lord. I love this passage, but there is a key phrase we can take out and apply to each moment of every single day, "for we walk by faith, not by sight."

My trouble with the cancer not returning was that I was living by sight, in a world in which I didn't want to live. I wanted to live with Christ in Heaven, but all around me was the world and was my life in this world. The reality is that I must keep a heavenly perspective, of Christ, while in this present life. I had been given overwhelming peace in my storm and anticipated life would get better in Heaven, and it will, but not now. I have the Word and the constant presence of the Spirit. That is all you and I will ever need to live by faith and not by sight, longing with each moment to be with Christ, but realizing there is purpose in this life and there is a reason the Lord has not called us home.

I must admit that to "walk by faith, not by sight" is something I am learning and praying for. We must remember, and I remind myself of this, that I am absolutely useless in this life if all I long for is Heaven. As a Christ-follower, I must long for, not just Heaven, but knowing God more each and every day. I must pursue Christ-likeness in reading, prayer, and fellowship; and maybe most of all sharing Christ with all I know. This world needs Christ and you and I are on a mission to plant seeds and harvest as the Spirit directs.

Remember, "walk by faith, not by sight!"

5

Will You Forget Me?

"'How long, O LORD? Will you forget me forever? ... I will sing to the Lord, because he has dealt bountifully with me."

~ Psalm 13:1a, 6

O ur number one hope in prayer is that our prayers are answered. Sometimes we wait years for prayers to be answered. They say hindsight is 20/20, that when we look back we can see how things worked out. David has hindsight in Psalm 13. Take a moment to read through Psalm 13 and as you read, consider how David's perspective changes.

David starts off in anguish, a theme of many of the psalms, and truly a theme in many of our lives. He is wondering why the Lord seems to have forgotten him. As you may have said through the trials of your life, "How long, O Lord?" So often in these desperate times, we take out our angst on the Lord. Deep down we know He is going to answer; we know He is ultimately in charge, but still, we wonder. If you are like me you have definitely said with David, "Will you forget me forever? How long will you hide your face from me?" We feel like we have been abandoned to the depths of our own soul and feel that our soul is the only thing that we can depend on. We feel God has forgotten us.

David continues in desperation even getting to the point of feeling he will die eternally apart from the Lord. In verse 3 he says, "Consider and answer me, O Lord my God; light up my eyes, lest I sleep the sleep of death." He worries that his enemy may be triumphant over him. I am sure we have all had our own "enemies," or people out to get us. We can just imagine lying on the floor with them looming over us, "I have prevailed over him," (Psalm 13:4) like a boxer standing over his defeated opponent. A horrific thought for sure! In a moment of desperation, we may feel very much like that defeated boxer, as if our lives had become a total knock out, an entire arena looking at our defeat. And the crowd defeating us with their taunts and derisions.

Yet, God's timing is always perfect. David has been suffering for who knows how long and then he remembers that God is on his side, and he has absolutely nothing to fear. It's like he is getting up from the mat in the boxing ring to look in his enemies' eyes thinking, "But I have trusted in [God's] steadfast love; my heart shall rejoice in your salvation" (Psalm 13:5). Knowing that almighty God is on his side, David realizes that he can face his present situation with the strength and courage to bring glory to the Lord and victory over his cause through the Lord.

When you were suffering, you were down on the mat. The situation seemed as if all would end, that even God had abandoned you. But in that one moment God whispers in your ear, "I will never leave you nor forsake you" (Hebrews 13:5). And again, in verse 6, the author of Hebrews quotes Psalm 118:6; "The Lord is on my side; I will not fear. What can man do to me?" The Lord gave you the strength to rise from the mat of the boxing ring surrounded by your enemy and the jeering crowds. And the reminder of who God is and His present faithfulness to you inspires you to keep pressing on in faith. Literally, what can any one person, or any one political or social group do to you? Christ is on your side; there is nothing to fear, fret, or worry about.

As you rise from the mat and see that the storm has subsided for a time, how will your prayers change? David started Psalm 13 wondering where God is and realizing that God had never left. God never lost control, and will provide an answer and relief when

He wills. Will you sing to the Lord with David, "he has dealt bountifully with me?" Will you sing even if the storm has exacted such a mighty toll on your life?

Will you trust the Lord to raise you up?

6

We Have Left Everything and Followed

"Jesus said, 'Truly, I say to you, there is no one who has left house or brothers or sisters or mother or father or children or lands, for my sake and for the gospel.'"

~ Mark 10:29

---◆---

As a history lover, I study history and am amazed by the lives, wealth, and power of the few over the course of human history. So few had so much, and yet from a material perspective, in the Western World, we are living extraordinary lives through the epochs of time. There is no culture in all of world history that has been more educated or more prosperous than ours. When we look at history, there is no civilization that has had it better than ours. In some ways, many poor people in our society are more comfortable than many kings and leaders of ancient history, even in the poor in the West are more comfortable than any peasant in centuries past. We live as if we have worked for our own prosperity, taking it for granted. We feel we are entitled to it, that it was all by our hand.

Consider your financial and relational position in life at the moment. Think about where you fit in terms of third world countries, true poverty of literally having absolutely nothing, and how regular people have lived throughout history with very little. Let's say Jesus is coming to town, think hypothetically with me for a moment, and you two plan on meeting over coffee. You both sit down, coffee in hand, and you have one question for Him, just one that has been pressing your mind and heart for months, if not years. Jesus agrees to answer your question.

You ask, "Good Teacher, what must I do to inherit eternal life?"

Jesus takes a sip and asks you, "Do you know what is required to follow me? Do you love God? Do you obey God?"

You confidently reply, "Of course, I have done all of those things. I have not done anything terrible in my entire life." Christ leans over and says,

"Yes, you've done all those things. There is, however, one thing you lack."

"What, Lord, do I lack?" You ask. Thinking you had done all that was required for eternal life, you are surprised that you are lacking in anything. You have done so much, and have been so good.

Christ replies, "Sell all that you have and give to the poor, and you will have treasure in heaven, and come follow me."

At first, you sit there stunned for a moment. In your mind you are thinking, "Wait, I have done so much." No words come to your mouth; you just cannot believe these words. After a few breaths, you dwell on what Jesus has said. You consider what He is saying. "Sell everything? Give everything to the poor?" Jesus' words are stinging because they are so drastic, seemingly unrealistic for the life you live, the work you do, the influence you have in your community. After a few minutes, your head still spinning, you get up, shake Jesus' hand, and walk away.

You just could not do it. Jesus was asking for everything. You were fine following Jesus, but only to a certain extent. You could be a disciple of Christ, but what Jesus was asking was too much.

I put you into the situation of the rich young ruler in Mark 12. The disciples are around Jesus as He tells the parable, and at the end, they are astonished. The thought going through their mind is,

"How do I get into the kingdom? How am I saved?" Like the disciples, it is a thought we have all had, "How do I get to Heaven?", the kingdom of God.

Calling out the rich young ruler, Jesus says, "It is easier for a camel to go through the eye of a needle than for a rich person to enter the kingdom of God" (Mark 10:25). The picture is almost hilarious, a camel going through the eye of a needle. If you held a needle up to a camel, you would not be able to see the needle. The disciples don't understand what Jesus is thinking. Jesus is saying it is very, very difficult.

But is Jesus saying that rich people cannot enter the kingdom? In the 21st century, we look at this rich young ruler and do not consider our wealth and position in comparison to his. We look at the rich young ruler and consider him way beyond our own wealth. The reality though for us is that we are the rich young ruler. For most in the Western World, we have wealth and comfort beyond anything the disciples could ever have imagined. Most of us in some part of our world, our job, our community have a strong position, we lead or control something. It is a tough thought to own, "I am the rich young ruler."

Hope is not lost though, because as we think about ourselves in the parable, Jesus gave us the answer, "Sell all you have, give to the poor, and follow me." What is Jesus really asking of us? Is he really asking us to sell everything, giving everything to the poor? You'll be glad to know the answer is "no."

But the answer is even more drastic; it deals with our hearts. The rich young ruler was unable to rip the hold his possessions and his position had on him. He just could not do it. He was unwilling to give up what he held in his heart for the sake of Christ.

Could you? Would you be willing to pray and lay down everything you own at the feet of Jesus, relinquishing control over it? Do you even know what is holding your heart? I ask that of myself as I ask it of you.

One of the greatest gifts I received from my trial was the perspective of this very thing. I felt as if I had lost everything I owned, every relationship I had, my job, my position, everything, save for Christ. I didn't really lose any physical possession in my life, but what I lost was the hold my material possessions had on me. I still lived in my home, my possessions were still there, my relationships were strengthened, I still had a job, and an expanded ministry in the church. There was a key element though, Christ held my heart, not my possessions. My relationship with Christ means everything to me, absolutely everything. I ended an interview for my church's "God at Work" series, right after I had finished radiation, saying, "I have lost everything, but Christ." This should be the rallying cry in our lives in the 21st century, not just in suffering, but in all parts of life.

You may be thinking to yourself that you just could not give it all up. Even today, I still sometimes think I cannot do it either because I know there are things in my life that my heart is holding onto. But Jesus tells His disciples something extraordinary in sacrificing ourselves for Him.

He says in Mark 10:27, "Jesus looked at them and said, 'With man it is impossible, but not with God. For all things are possible with God.'" My perspective was not mine, but it was His. It was His extraordinary work in my life that allowed that viewpoint, and I know if you genuinely see Him over all those things that hold our hearts, He will allow you to believe that all things are possible with every fiber of your lives.

Putting everything on the line for Christ is completely antithetical to the western world. This is going to sound odd, but bear with me a moment, it seems countercultural because it is, and that is the point. In a precious end to this convicting, heavy parable is a gem that we can hold onto if we are holding onto Christ. He finishes the section, "But many who are first will be last, and the last first" (Mark 10:31). Our story is not done and someday we will see this entire world turn upside down for Christ. What presently makes sense now is not going to make any sense under the rule and reign of Christ when He returns.

At what cost for Christ? EVERYTHING!

7

Established by the Lord

"The steps of man are established by the Lord, when he delights in his way; though he fall, he shall not be cast headlong, for the Lord upholds his hand. I have been young, and now am old, yet I have not seen the righteous forsaken or his children begging for bread."

~ Psalm 37:23-25

———•◆•———

Our storms change our plans, our goals, and our lives. Many times, temporarily, sometimes permanently. Psalm 37 has enamored me for years and I pray you will take a moment to read through it and consider what it says about the Lord. In your past, have you ever decided to do something, go somewhere, make plans, and yet all of them have changed? How have you felt?

It can be so very disappointing to think about something we would have loved to have happened only to find it lost when plans are altered. As hard and disappointing as it is, it is beautiful to know the Lord has changed your path, that He is so directly involved in your life, that He wants the absolute best for you, for His absolute glory.

As we realized in our past suffering we will fall, we will fail, we will sin again and again and again, but the reality is that life will never be so bad, so lost, so forlorn that all hope is lost. Not a single thing happens that the Lord has not allowed through His hand,

and as David writes in the psalm, "The Lord upholds his hand." The Lord is going to lift you up out of whatever situation you are in to bring you to a greater place, even if it does not seem so in the moment.

You have suffered in this life, and here you are. I pray you are moving on from the storms of your trial to the calm of the present. As the Lord calls us in our trials, so He calls us in the time after our suffering and says in Psalm 37:7 to "Be still before the Lord and wait patiently for him: fret not yourself over the one who prospers in his way, over the man who carries out evil devices." Waiting patiently can be one of the most difficult things we could do in our Christian life. We trust and know the Lord is going to work. We trust and know God is going to provide a path and purpose in the days and journeys of our lives. While it is difficult to wait, we can trust that God is going to work beyond our beliefs, beyond our wants. The great truth is, we know He is going to fulfill His place for us and in us.

He will make His plans, your plans and His paths, your paths!

8

Gospel Going

"How then will they call on him in who they have not believed? And how are they to believe in him of whom they have never heard? And how are they to hear without someone preaching? And how are they to preach unless they are sent? As it is written, 'How beautiful are the feet of those who preach the good news!'"

~ **Romans 10: 14-15**

How did you come to know of Christ's saving grace? What is your story? Your testimony? Do you remember where you were when you came to salvation in Jesus Christ as Lord and Savior? Do you remember who was a big influence in bringing you to Christ?

You may not know it, but someone took the time in word or deed, or both, to share and live out a saved life in Christ so that someone else (you) might also know Christ. Someone wanted to share their story of what Christ did in their lives for the sake of your eternal soul. Someone loved you so much they were willing to take the risk of sharing Jesus Christ so that your life might be saved. You needed to hear the gospel from someone, to see the work of Christ in another's life, to know that Christ was serious about your salvation.

The Lord is preparing you to share your story, of God's work in your life. And remember what Paul says in Romans 10:17, "So faith comes from hearing, and hearing through the word of Christ."

There are no chance encounters in sharing the gospel, whether successful or not, each is God-ordained to happen. Remember we may be the ones planting the gospel, growing the gospel, or leading someone to salvation. God has a plan for us, and He gives us a part in that plan in expanding the gospel.

God's work in your life is a part of seeing the gospel at work! Go tell your story as a testament of His work in you!

9

A Path Attended

"He leads the humble in what is right, and teaches the humble his way."

~ Psalm 25:9

———◦♦———

Psalm 25, as a whole, is an excellent prayer to prepare for a trial, during a trial, and after a trial. Would it not be wise for us to always be prepared for the Lord to work in ways unimaginable, including those difficult days? David is wisely lifting up this path of suffering, and truly any path in life, up to the Lord, knowing the Lord will have His way directing David's path for God's glory. Traveling paths of old followed the geography like rivers; rarely were they straight and rarely were they easy. With many twists and turns, ups and downs we move through life to our final destination as Christ-followers, Heaven. It is these twisted paths that David writes of in this prayer. Take a moment to read and pray through Psalm 25.

It would seem odd to say that having exited a trial we should prepare for the next trial, but as I hear often from friends, my pastor, and at church, "You are either entering a trial or exiting a trial." It is the sad reality of our human state that suffering, because of sin, is an absolute for all people. This is especially true for the Christ-follower where even Christ told us in John 16:33, "In the world you will have tribulation." Christ Himself was known as a "man of sorrows" (Isaiah 53:3). If Christ should carry the mantle of "man of sorrows" and suffering, should not we as His children prepare at all times for any trials to come our way?

David speaks a wonderful and beautiful universal truth that we must hold onto always: the Lord is in absolute control during all times of life, the good and bad. In verse 1 of Psalm 25 we have no idea of David's particular situation, though it is accepted he is entering a time of suffering. Instead of looking to himself or his situation, he lifts his soul up to the Lord in complete trust of the Lord's role and sovereignty over every part of his life. Knowing that God is always sovereign should draw our eyes off all parts of our lives to look at the Lord and to consider how the Lord is going to use the situation for His glory!

The Bible should be a constant companion for us this side of Heaven. No doubt there are a great many books that help draw us to the Lord, but the bulk of our time should be spent in the Word, for those are the words of God, and any other words are the mere words of men. David, a devoted reader of the Word, knows that the Lord is going to take him down roads he has never imagined and is praying that he might know the ways the Lord goes. He wants to know God, His nature, His character, His way of life. While David is living his life, he wants to live in a way that pleases the Lord, knowing who the Lord is and how the Lord works. David wants God in His life no matter what path the Lord will take him on. And even not knowing the paths ahead in his life, he places his trust in the Lord. He says in Psalm 25:5, "Lead me in your truth and teach me, for you are the God of my salvation, for you I wait all day long." David's goal is not to survive in life, but to thrive in the Lord, and in thriving in the Lord, David knows He will survive whatever dark paths are ahead.

Later in the psalm, David discusses a character trait that is the primary position he must hold as a part of God's family, humility. David holds humility up as the premier attitude and position in trusting his present and future to the Lord. He knows who God is and who he is as a man. When it comes to a position before the Lord, as humans, we have no standing without Christ. David allows God His rightful position. This is His world, and He should work in and through it as He wills, as He desires, without question. David shares this truth in Psalm 25:9, "He leads the humble in what is right, and teaches the humble his way." David is saying that if you want to know what is right and correct, what is true and real, you must lay aside yourself for knowing the One who is all right, all correct, all true and all real, for all time. David understands God and he wants his readers to understand and delight in God that the paths of life, no matter how high and low they go, may be put in their proper place before God's throne.

I pray that in your suffering there were a few faithful believers who walked that road with you.* I was entirely blessed with such true and honorable companions, the utmost being the Lord Himself, whose intimate presence and guide was a comfort during such pain. You may have learned and understood through your own trial that there is not a gift as great as the presence and friendship of the Lord. He says later in the passage, "The friendship of the Lord is for those who fear him, and he makes known to them his covenant" (Psalm 25:14). Imagine you calling God your friend as David does in this psalm. What a glorious thought to call God friend. God was present on David's paths of life, so is He on the paths we face in this life, but especially in these distinct storms.

The paths of our lives will take on many forms and how we approach them and who we approach them with will make all the difference for all those crazy twists and turns, the ups and downs, the lights and darks. This time of rest after the storm is an excellent time to start training our body and soul for the next trial. It is a time of clarity, of trusting the Lord, of evaluating our situation and path and moving ahead in our relationship with the Lord. Knowing how He works makes all the difference in any part of life.

Pray over your time out of the storm, that you will stand with the Lord hand in hand embracing the roads of life He has in store with and for you.

10

Truth in the Night

"Truly, truly, I say to you, unless one is born again, he cannot see the kingdom of God."

~ John 3:3

———— ◆ ————

The Jewish religious leaders were ever present and ever critical of Jesus from the beginning of His ministry to His resurrection. They hung on every word He said, always critical of what He said and the miracles He did. They were the experts in Israel, and Jesus did not fit their narrative and desire for a political messiah.

Picture this seen from the Book of John, in the crowd stands a Pharisee and member of the Sanhedrin, intently listening to each word Jesus says, honestly considering and taking it all to heart. His name is Nicodemus. He is curious as to the truth of what Jesus is doing, and unlike the other leaders, sought Jesus out to understand the truth about Jesus and what He was saying about salvation. Nicodemus is pondering, "Who is this Jesus? What is He about? How is someone saved?" These are questions we have all had. But Nicodemus' questions are pressing, and his heart and mind will not rest until he gets his answers.

Nicodemus comes to Jesus at night. As a Pharisee and member of the Sanhedrin, he is essentially going to meet with the enemy. He fears what other religious leaders would say. He is putting his job, his prestige, in some ways his entire life on the line to honestly understand who Jesus is. It is very much like our brothers and sisters in Christ living in countries hostile to Christianity, who are willing to sacrifice everything to hear a sermon or to pray with another believer.

Jesus welcomes Nicodemus into the place where Jesus is staying. Nicodemus knows he is taking a risk meeting with Jesus, but is willing to do anything to get answers to his questions. Nicodemus asks his questions towards Jesus regarding salvation, the questions that are deep within his heart and mind, but Jesus' answers confuse him. He does not understand.

Jesus says that to be saved a man must be born again, which makes Nicodemus think that he must reenter his mother's womb and literally and physically be born again. Being a Pharisee, Nicodemus is used to knowing all the answers to all the questions. Like the other religious leaders of his day, and many of us in churches today, parading around like peacocks, thinking we know everything and have life all figured out. Compared to Jesus we are all at a disadvantage and will be humbled.

Jesus clarifies that "unless one is born of the water and the Spirit, he cannot enter the kingdom of God." He continues in verses 7 and 8, "You must be born again. The wind blows where it wishes, and you do not know where it comes from or where it goes. So it is with everyone who is born of the Spirit." Jesus is saying that the movement of the wind is a mystery to mankind and so is the work of the Spirit. It is not something that we can entirely understand. The Spirit is going to work as He wills, not as we understand.

Nicodemus in his naivete, like us in our ignorance, is wondering, "How can this be?" This does not make sense to the smart, intellectual, emphatic leader, but he sets an example for us all in that when it comes to Christ, there is no time when we can entirely say that we understand one hundred percent of everything about God and His Word. And everything in salvation comes down to

Christ, absolutely everything. John will write later in 1 John 5:1, "Everyone who believes that Jesus is the Christ has been born of God and everyone who loves the Father loves whoever has been born of him." Jesus is the answer to every question Nicodemus has, and every question you may have.

Jesus was gracious, willing to take any question Nicodemus had. Even though Nicodemus came searching, the Spirit was already at work in Nicodemus' heart to bring him to Christ. But Jesus' graciousness also holds a strong truth that has split families and hearts ever since, and Nicodemus has to consider the implications. Jesus said in verse 3 that one must be born again. Jesus is now addressing the "who". Nicodemus is wondering who is going to save him. Jesus, trying to relate to Nicodemus, shares an example that Nicodemus would understand. He chooses Moses as an example. Going back to the book of Numbers, Jesus tells him in John 3:14-15, "And as Moses lifted up the serpent in the wilderness, so must the Son of Man be lifted up, that whoever believes in him may have eternal life." Nicodemus knew the passage from Numbers where many of the Israelites were bit by snakes because they demonstrated their unbelief in God by speaking out against Him, even though they had seen the Lord's protection and provision towards them for years. God directs Moses to create a bronze staff of a serpent and a person dying of a snake bite can look at it and be healed. The connection is that in order to be saved a person must look to Christ. In that last moment, Nicodemus is confronted with his salvation; His name is Jesus, and the choice to believe and follow is his.

As a Pharisee, Nicodemus is realizing the gravity of who Jesus is. Jesus did not fit the narrative of the religious leaders, that Messiah would come for an earthly kingdom, but instead, He came for a spiritual kingdom, His kingdom. Jesus' kingdom was not of this world, just as His salvation is not of this world.

The reality of salvation is that it is all about Christ. Unlike all other religions, there is nothing you or I could ever do to save ourselves. In every other religion, including some that society places under the Christian umbrella, if we want to be saved, we have to work our way to God. The reality of biblical Christianity is that

God came down to us from the splendors of Heaven to the dregs of this world, to save us. Paul writes in Ephesians 2:4-6, "But God being rich in mercy, because of the great love with which he loved us, even when we were dead in our trespasses, made us alive together with Christ—by grace you have been saved—and raised us up with him and seated us with him in the heavenly places in Christ Jesus."

We each have a choice: Are we going to trust Christ as our Lord and Savior or are we going to handle life and eternity on our own? The time to accept Christ as Lord and Savior is now, not tomorrow, not when life calms down, not when you figure things out, not when you feel clean enough or good enough, but NOW! You and I know in our suffering that we are not necessarily given tomorrow, and time is of the essence. If you are not a Christian, how prepared are you to accept Jesus as your Lord and Savior?

People are desperate for salvation, for the pain of their souls to be healed. If you are a follower of Christ, the Lord has done a mighty work in your life through your own trial. You have a story to tell of God's working in your life and how He worked in your own tribulations. Nicodemus was given the truth about his state as an unbeliever; Jesus gave him the truth about how to be saved. We can rejoice today that Nicodemus is a brother to you, living with Christ in Heaven. Who is your future brother and sister in Christ that you need to reach out to with the gospel of Christ? One must be born again, in Christ alone.

How prepared are you to share the gospel with those who are seeking salvation?

11

Truth in the Night Postscript

"For God so loved the world that he gave his only Son, that whoever believes in him should not perish but have eternal life. For God did not send his son into the world to condemn the world, but in order that the world might be saved through him. Whoever believes in him is not condemned, but whoever does not believe is condemned already, because he has not believed in the name of the only Son of God."

~ John 3:16-18

I did not neglect to include John 3:16-18 in the entry, "Truth in the Night," but wanted to focus on the interaction of Nicodemus and Jesus outside of what most Christ-followers know. I can only speak for myself, but you may find yourself like me. When I encounter a verse I'm familiar with, I tend to gloss over it, ignoring the great truth written in it. These verses from John 3 are often coffee mug, t-shirt, or tattoo verses, so familiar we forget the meaning. I dare say that we have taken the depth out of many a verse over the years.

I want to pull out a couple of things from these verses that may have lost their meaning and importance over the years.

Consider the sacrifice of God. For eternity past the Father, Son, and Holy Spirit existed together, always together, never apart. There was no need for them to break ever, but then humanity chose to split from their Creator. We chose sin over God. In choosing sacrifice, Jesus the Son of God left the throne room in Heaven for our sin-tainted world and gave Himself willingly so that the relationship between God and His people might be restored. Our relationship with God was returned to the rightful place in heaven. That restoration happens only through Christ as John writes in verse 18, "Whoever believes in him is not condemned, but whoever does not believe is condemned already because he has not believed in the name of the only Son of God."

In that salvation and restored relationship, we come to our place with God in Heaven. The benefits of following Christ are knowing God personally and actively, secured in salvation through His Son by the Spirit, and a place in Heaven, "eternal life." Our world is so temporary, so changing with the winds of time, that we do not truly and honestly know permanence aside from the work of Christ in our lives. Eternal life is a permanency of residence and outcome of our eternal relationship with God Almighty!

And the reality of our world is that people believe there are many ways to "God," but as Nicodemus is learning, as the Roman world will learn through the works of Peter, Paul, the Apostles, and the many disciples and missionaries throughout the ages is that the answer to knowing God is only through Jesus Christ. For many, it is a hard truth to swallow, but it is the truth nonetheless and we have to accept that truth if we are to be saved. As Christ says to Nicodemus about the light of life in Christ in this dark world, "but whoever does what is true comes to the light, so that it may be clearly seen that his works have been carried out in God" (John 3:21).

God wrote every word in the Bible for a purpose. May you and I read each verse, not for the sake of a quick read, but to be read for maximum impact in our lives. May we each take a verse and chew, distill, and absorb it to make the truth of Christ more permanent, meaningful, and personal in our life with Jesus Christ.

12

Turning a New Leaf

"And whatever you do, in word or deed, do everything in the name of the Lord Jesus, giving thanks to God the Father through him."

~ Colossians 3:17

———◆———

The phrase "turning a new leaf" is common in the Western World, meaning turning to a new page in a book, starting over, going down a different path. Trials and tribulations provide us with a unique opportunity to turn a page in our lives and to open to the freshness of a new chapter in life. Few people in our world, believers and unbelievers alike, take the opportunity to open a new page, to start a new part of the story of our lives, to take a risk and leave the past where it is and start on a new path of life. Of the many blessings the Lord gives us in suffering, this is one of the best. The Lord is not giving us a chance to start life over, but to redirect our lives in ways toward Him, in ways toward a better life in Christ. The thought of pursuing a new path should excite us all. It is a new part of our lives, an unexpected, sometimes thrilling part of our lives. To know the Lord is walking each step with us should bring great encouragement.

In your suffering, you were in a deep, dark valley. The Lord, in your recovery, is calling you out of that valley. As He takes you out of the valley, as the light slowly returns, you see the glorious forest around you. As you walk, it is slow-going, but enthralling to see things from a new perspective, to breathe a fresh new breath. Eventually, over time, you get to the top of the mountain and you look out on where you have been. You turn and the Lord takes you down a new road out of that place, onto a new, better, closer life with Him. There is a fork in the road and you could go back to the old life, or a comparable path, or you could chart out, with the Lord leading the way, into brand new territory.

Can you think back on your life and see times and events when you have turned the page in life? Looking back over your life is like reading a novel, and you turn the page not knowing where the story is going, but excited to see where it all may go. This is the place you stand at this moment, waiting for the page to turn and to start a new part of life. The storm is over, you and the Lord have started a journey out of the valley. You are standing on the beach wondering what has transpired since you were out at sea struggling, and here you are moving out of these places back toward a new life. The wonderful thing is you and the Lord get an opportunity to journey into and build a new life, whatever that may look like.

As you look toward a new life, consider the admonitions of Paul in Colossians 3:17: "And whatever you do, in word or deed, do everything in the name of the Lord Jesus, giving thanks to God the Father through him." You get to look at life from a new perspective. Whatever new outlook you have on life and your walk with the Lord, consider what you are doing for Him. In this new life, this "new normal" He is helping you build; it is essential that you build a life with all eyes focused on the Lord. Paul says, "Do everything in the name of the Lord Jesus." From big to small we are encouraged in everything we do for the glory of God.

One year after I had my second brain surgery to remove the cancer, I decided that since we do not know the number of our days that I would do something at the top of my bucket list. I chose to go skydiving! It was a way of celebrating what the Lord had done, taking a fun risk, and starting over. It was so fulfilling that my dad and I have done it every year on that date for five years now, and while we jump, my mom is holding her breath every year for us, praying us to safety.

I did not intentionally skydive to symbolically turn a new page, but the third year we went, we met Michelle from Texas who was skydiving to turn a new leaf. She was in California for work and decided that she was going to skydive to start life over after a divorce and the death of her son. My mom spoke with her while my dad and I did our dive, and we came back to hear her harrowing life story and how she was going back to Texas with a new outlook and *Anchored in the Storm* in her mind. The Lord is allowing you to face life anew, refreshed with a new perspective after your trial.

While you may have a new outlook and a new path in your life as the storm calms, you must remember you are a Christ-follower, and being a Christ-follower, you have a special way of living. And Paul reminds us that "Whatever you do, in word or deed, do everything in the name of the Lord Jesus, giving thanks to God the Father through him." What a thought that in every movement of our body, every thought in our mind, every word spoken, is to be done in the name of the Lord, in thankfulness, all for His glory. I confess that this is not easy in a world where we are to think of ourselves first and that everything we do must be for ourselves. Take a moment and review a normal day in your life. Most of the things we do are fairly meaningless: eating, drinking, moving from one place to another around our homes and workplaces. Paul reminds the Colossians that every part of life, in word and deed, is for the Lord, and He is even more specific in I Corinthians 10:31, "So, whether you eat or drink, or whatever you do, do all to the glory of God." He says, "whatever you do," it is to be done for His glory; it is to bring attention and praise to Him.

The road out of the valley, like the road into the valley, may not be the easiest, but with each step you take, you turn a new page, start a new chapter, take a different path. Remember, the Lord has given you this new life. By His hand we have "life, and breath, and all things" (Acts 17:25), and thus He should always be at the forefront of everything we do.

13

Foxes Have Holes

"And Jesus said to him, 'Foxes have holes, and birds of the air have nests, but the Son of Man has nowhere to lay his head.'"

~ Luke 9:58

I have lived in Southern California my entire life, and my family has been here for close to 150 years. It is my home. People of Southern California tend to be fairly shallow, fake, and love when other people comment positively about how great their life is, how nice they look, and how great their family is. You could say we like to live the "perfect" life here, while we all know it is all a façade. We are friends with certain people because they are like us, or we can get something from them, or being around them makes us look good or significant. And we choose not to be friends with certain people because they are not like us, or do not fit into our version of life.

Sadly, we do the same in the church. Everyone is great on Sunday mornings. Our photoshopped holiday photos convey great "blessings" from above, and we like our living areas well-manicured and beautiful, as a "good Christian home" looks like. Not a hair or blade of grass is out of place, either on your head or on your lawn. (And I have quite a thinning patch on the back of my head, thanks to my genes and thanks to my cancer!) In our daily lives everything is "great."

Yet, when we close our front doors, we know that all is not right. Our hearts are attached to the world, to the comforts of our world, and the pleasure we get from people complimenting us regarding our "perfect" lives. This world is home to us, and we build and beautify every aspect of our lives because we think we are going to be here "forever." The sense of competition for the best creates a subtle, but dangerous sin of envy and jealousy. It is hard to avoid when the comforts and pleasures of this life are all around us, outside our homes, inside our homes, and inside our souls.

The gift in suffering for the believer is trials. These trials tend to take this world and our worldly pursuits away and we get this beautiful time with the Lord, just us and Him. My time with the Lord in my own trial was such a beautiful blessing, but I have realized as the trial ended that those old envies returned slowly, but they sadly did return. The pain of our trials creates a time of immense intimacy with the Lord. But after the storm the world system that we have adapted to comes back like a vengeance, and in some ways, another fight (against this world) is on.

How does Jesus respond to this world and the way we live in this world? What would He say to us today, in a world obsessed with materialism, the life we pretend to have, entitlement, and the thin façade over our lives? Let's look at Luke 9:57-62 to see what Jesus says about our lives.

"As they were going along the road, someone said to him, 'I will follow you wherever you go.' And Jesus said to him, 'Foxes have holes, and birds of the air have nests, but the Son of Man has nowhere to lay his head.' To another he said, 'Follow me.' But he said, 'Lord, let me first go and bury my father.' And Jesus said to him, 'Leave the dead to bury their own dead. But as for you, go and proclaim the kingdom of God.' Yet another said, 'I will follow you, Lord, but let me first say farewell to those at my home.' Jesus said to him, 'No one who puts his hand to the plow and looks back is fit for the kingdom of God.'"

Jesus is traveling with an unknown number of people, but Luke shares Jesus' response to three of these travelers. The passage involves three life statements from three different people as they traveled on the road. Jesus' responses put our lives in perspective when it comes to calling Him Lord and being faithful to Him. What cost is there in following Jesus? And what holds our hearts?

Imagine the heat of the sun, the cool breeze, the grind of the dirt as a crowd walks with Jesus from one town to the next.

The first comment and commitment from the passage will resonate with you. The first person says, "I will follow you wherever you go." Have you ever said that before? I know I have. As Christ-followers it is what we say. "Jesus, where you go, I will go." But deep down is this true? Would you truly be willing to go wherever Jesus goes? Would you be willing to do what He has asked of you, no matter how hard and inconvenient it might be? Would you be willing to go with Him wherever? Would you be willing to give up your beautiful life on this earth if Jesus required? It's easier to say, "I will follow you wherever you go," than it is to actually do it.

Jesus must have given this traveler a courteous smile before he responds. Jesus turns His face to look the traveler in the eyes and replies, "Foxes have holes, and birds of the air have nests, but the Son of Man has nowhere to lay his head." Every creature has his home, his place of existence, but in this world, there is no adequate place for the Son of God. The sad reality of the world from Genesis 3 to present day is that while God is in charge of the universe and has ultimate authority, Satan has power over the world. Paul describes the power of Satan and the role we played in following him in Ephesians 2:1-3: "And you were dead in the trespasses and sins in which you once walked, following the course of this world, following the prince of the power of the air (Satan), the spirit that is now at work in the sons of disobedience—among whom we all once lived in the passions of our flesh, carrying out the desires of the body and the mind, and were by nature children of wrath, like the rest of mankind." (Parentheses for Satan mine)

Jesus temporarily gave up a face to face present relationship with the Lord to be on this earth. He came to a world under the control of Satan to save you. He gave up the glories and splendors of Heaven to dwell among us, in a world where He officially did not belong. This world was made for humans, not for the Son of God, and this world is the way it is because of our sin. It is a world entirely tainted and dominated by sin, not the holiness Jesus knows. Yet, Jesus gave up everything to come down to this earth, to suffer, to die, all for the sake of saving His beloved—you and me.

They continue walking and Jesus turns His head and tells another traveler, "Follow me." Amazingly this second traveler has an excuse, "Lord, let me first go and bury my father." The reality is this man's father had not died. This common statement of the day meant that he wanted to wait until he had his inheritance and once that is in hand then he will follow Jesus. Jesus was not going to even consider the traveler's excuse for a moment.

He responds, "Leave the dead to bury their own dead. But as for you, go and proclaim the kingdom of God." Jesus is not trying to be harsh with the man but is calling the man out. How committed is the man to the call of Christ? Jesus had just called the man and said, "Follow me." Jesus does not say that to anyone but has chosen a select few in this world to be His followers, though Jesus does desire the salvation of all mankind, His creation. He isn't going to take any excuses from anyone, especially those He has called to salvation.

It's like the conversation Jesus and Peter have after Jesus' resurrection. Peter was questioning Jesus about the life ahead for each of the disciples. Peter was particularly looking at John, wondering what his days looked like. Jesus responds with an exhortation to Peter, one we can all use. Jesus replies in John 21:22, "If it is my will that he remain until I come, what is that to you? You follow me!" Jesus has a plan, place, and purpose for each of us. It's a plan by the hand of God for each of us individually. It's not our place to look at another and ask God why we got something different than someone else. We do not know this second traveler's response, but Jesus' strong encouragement must have driven the man to continue on this path of faith.

The third traveler was listening to the discussion of the previous two travelers and appeared to hang on every word that Jesus said. He's desperate to enter the conversation and tells Jesus, "I will follow you, Lord." He has heard what Jesus has said to those who want to follow Jesus and it sounds like he is in. "But let me first say farewell to those at my home." He must have missed the two previous conversations where Jesus pretty much says, "Follow Me and that is it. Period. Done." It seems to be a thing that you wonder, is it not good for the man to say goodbye to his family and friends? Jesus replies, "No one who puts his hand to the plow and looks back is fit for the kingdom of God." Jesus says the man is looking back on his past life, holding onto what was, and not looking ahead to what is in Christ. A farmer who looks back while plowing is going to cut a crooked path for his seeds and that is useless.

These three travelers must have walked along with jaws dropped open, seemingly with defeated and conflicted hearts. They wanted Jesus and … successful, beautiful, comfortable lives; financial stability, and mostly praise. If we are honest with ourselves, we want Jesus "plus," not just Jesus alone. Jesus is saying, "When you follow Me, you follow Me." What we struggle to understand in this passage is that our hearts are so stuck in this world that we find it almost impossible to fully follow Jesus. He is interested in all of us, but the reality is that we are not interested in all of Him. If we look at our lives, we are no different than these three travelers. We are all holding onto something that distracts from our relationship with Jesus.

As we move from the storm to the calm, our hearts are challenged to keep our eyes and hearts focused completely and absolutely on Jesus. The good thing about our suffering is that it was a time when the world's hold on our hearts was taken away and we were able to purely see Jesus without the distractions of this world. But we are not suffering right now. Life is supposed to get better, yet we see the world still holds part of our hearts. Deep down we know there are things we need to bring before the Lord.

In Luke 9, Jesus reminds us of Himself, there is no place on this earth He can call home. He had no possessions to speak of. When He ascended to Heaven, there was nothing of His that He left behind because He had nothing here on earth. No place and no thing to call His own. When Jesus came down to bring us salvation, He left everything in Heaven, focused on His goal of bringing the gospel, dying on the cross, and raising Himself from the dead. Jesus even goes as far in John 4:34 to say, "My food is to do the will of Him who sent me and to accomplish his work." He is so focused on accomplishing the Father's will that to Him even food is meaningless in comparison to the will of God. Everything we hold dear and close to our hearts is meaningless compared to the call of Christ on our lives, in the storm, or on the shore.

For these three travelers, the issue is not what they possess, but what possesses them. Are they willing to give up everything to the Lord so the Lord may work as He wills through them? Are they willing to make life more authentic and real so others may see Jesus working in their lives as opposed to seeing a life that looks like it does not need Jesus? Are they willing to lay aside the life they want for true life in Christ knowing it may be hard and difficult, but also knowing the rewards to come far outweigh anything we presently know in this world? Are you willing to surrender and give up everything for Jesus?

Now is the time when you get to start a renewed and refreshed life. You get to rip your heart from this world and give it all to Christ. What is holding your heart back?

14

For the Sake of Christ

> *""For the sake of Christ, then, I am content with weaknesses, insults, hardships, persecutions, and calamities. For when I am weak, then I am strong."*
>
> ~ 2 Corinthians 12:10

———— ◆ ————

Have you ever read something, stopped for a moment, and had to go back and reread it, like, "Did I read that correctly? Who would say that? Am I really reading this?" It takes a moment to come to your senses to really clarify and understand what is being said. Paul, in the passage from 2 Corinthians, writes one of those statements where you take a moment, take a breath, shake a head, and go back to read it again. Who in their right mind would be willing to take on weakness, insult, hardship, persecution, and calamity? Who does this? Who is this person?

The answer is that Paul does. In his life he seemingly saw and did it all, including targeting and killing Christians across the Middle East. Paul's epic salvation in the book of Acts, the 13 letters he wrote, all tell of his travels around the Mediterranean world to spread the gospel. He was executed at the hands of Rome, all the while completely sold out to the Lord. Wherever the Lord led him, he went. Whatever the Lord wanted him to do, he did. There was no question in Paul's heart that he was the Lord's, and he willingly and patiently served the Lord wherever he went. Paul is an example for all of us to follow, but when looking at Paul as an example, we must remember that Paul is a human just like you and me. But Paul has an example in Christ, and he followed that example all the way to Rome to face execution for devotion to his savior

What does Paul see in Christ that would enable him to give up every seeming comfort in life? To call his suffering a joy? To willingly be imprisoned and executed for Christ? In Christ, Paul sees everything; in the world Paul sees nothing. I am not sure if I am at the point in my life and in my walk with Christ where I could say those words, "For the sake of Christ, then, I am content with _____" (Fill in whatever you're holding onto.) If Christ asked, Paul would be willing to take on traits that are the most invaluable traits our world wants. Our world looks with indignation upon contentment and weakness. Our world loves going after Christians. Our world loves persecuting those who choose to live lives with Christ in our present culture. Our world derides those who anticipate calamity in life. In every way, our world is against Christ and all that He is. The world does not want salvation; they do not want to know Him, and anyone associated with Christ must be targeted, that is the world's prerogative. This is the world we live in, and as followers of Christ we must prepare for when our soul is called out and we are questioned by Christ and the world, "What holds your heart?"

One goal God has in our suffering is to remove our attention and our hearts away from this world to Him and the things He delights in, in hopes that we will delight in those same things. In order to have a life in Christ worth anything, we have to make a sacrifice. We have to put ourselves, our comforts, even our lives on the line for the sake of Christ. Christ wants all of us, not all of us and _____ (again, you fill in the blank). He wants you and all of you and in giving everything you are to Him; you are getting everything you could ever want!

Considering the future ahead, what are you holding onto? What do you need to remove from your mind, from your heart, and from your life so Christ can have all of you? As you ponder the road ahead, in and out of suffering, are you willing to give up your strength, your possessions, your position, literally putting everything on the line all for Christ? Are you willing to be insulted and persecuted for being a Christian? Are you ready to be thrown out of your community and friendships? Are you ready to die for Christ?

Paul, being human just like us, might be thinking that he really doesn't want to lose his possessions, his health, or his life for anyone. We really don't want to hurt and be hurt for anyone. Paul has the right perspective in considering that if Christ is proclaimed, if people come to Christ because of your suffering, if your weakness makes Christ look strong, then it is all worth it. And as you consider life after your trial, consider what needs to be removed from your life so when the day comes, when your reputation is on the line, when your possessions are being taken, when you lose your job, when your heart is compromised, all for Christ, that you could stand there with a smile in your eyes and praise and proclaim, "For the sake of Christ!"

What is Christ worth in your life?

15

No ... Nothing

*"No, in all these things we are more than conquerors through him
who loved us. For I am sure that neither death nor life, nor angels nor
rulers, nor things present nor things to come, nor powers, nor height
nor depth, nor anything else in all creation, will be able to separate us
from the love of God in Christ Jesus our Lord."*

~ **Romans 8:37-39**

———•◆•———

Take a moment to read through Romans 8, one of the
most profound chapters in Romans. Romans is one of
the most profound books in the Bible. Did you read it?
Really, go back and read it! WOW! What is Paul saying in Romans 8? Essentially Paul is telling the Romans in verses
37-39, with God on your side there is no one and no thing to fear.
God's got this ... trust in Him.

Reflect for a minute on your past, particularly your past as a
Christ-follower. Think back on the times when someone was
against you, when you felt like you were being targeted for something you did or did not do, a viewpoint you held, a person you
supported, persecution or critical questions over your faith. The
reality is that yes, sometimes you and I can cause someone to be
against you, but for those times when there is nothing we did, what
goes through your mind as you wonder why someone is against
you? Why do they want you to fail? Is it for your faith? Is it because you belong to Christ?

Does it matter if you have done absolutely nothing to cause someone to be against you? Who is on your side every second, every minute, every hour of every day? God is! Paul writes, "No, in all these things we are more than conquerors through him who loved us. For I am sure that neither death nor life, nor angels nor rulers, nor things present nor things to come, nor powers, nor height nor depth, nor anything else in all creation, will be able to separate us from the love of God in Christ Jesus our Lord" (Romans 8:37-39). There is nothing in this world that can be against you if the Lord is on your side. Yes, there may be accusations, but who would dare take on the Lord? Does it matter who is against us if God is for us?

Our evil and sin-infected world is not a challenge for God. The world under the present dominion of Satan and his followers wants you to betray Christ, to turn away from Him who from the dawn of creation had a plan to rescue the people of the Lord. Satan wants to destroy every part of your relationship with Christ. The beautiful reality is that Satan has no power to do that. Yes, we can go through times when we focus less on Christ, read His Word less, pray less, spend time with our brothers and sisters less, which can all reduce our witness. At the end of the day, is there anything that can separate you from Christ, ever? No … nothing!

16

Calmed and Quieted

"O Lord, my heart is not lifted up; my eyes are not raised too high; I do not occupy myself with things too great and too marvelous for me. But I have calmed and quieted my soul, like a weaned child with its mother; like a weaned child my soul within me. O Israel, hope in the Lord from this time forth forevermore."

~ Psalm 131

———— ♦ ————

Life is not easy. That is the reality. We have good days and we have bad days. David is a rarity among the many biblical writers; while displaying such boldness in his faith, David demonstrates the emotions of his faith throughout his psalms. David brings us to an almost childlike, winsome place in our relationship with the Lord. Remember as a child how much it meant to sit on the lap of your mom or dad, or if you are a parent, how much it meant to your child just to be held by you, or to be embraced in security by a loved one. In those moments, you feel as if the world were at peace and nothing, in no way, could go wrong. All is well.

Like you as a child, like your child is with you, David reminds us that we are to look at God as a child does to his or her father and mother. There is a peace in being held in the arms of the Lord. No doubt there were times in your suffering when you felt completely incapable of moving from your position—your heart was down, your eyes could barely rise up from the hurt. There were no meaningful thoughts beyond your pain meandering about your mind, just suffering, and yet, you recalled the Lord, lifted your eyes to Him, and you were clutched in His arms as you endured the storm. And in that moment of knowing the Lord was present, all was calm, all was quiet, all was in order and secure.

The foundation of Psalm 131 rests in our deeply intimate relationship with the Lord and knowing the Lord will embrace us with the deepest of relationships. As David looks away from the Father to encounter life again, He reminds us, as He reminded Israel, that we must now and always, place our hope in the Lord.

Be as near to the Lord as a child is to a parent!

17

No Memory

"And no longer shall each one teach his neighbor and each his brother, saying, 'Know the Lord' for they shall all know me, from the least of them to the greatest, declares the Lord. For I will forgive their iniquity, and I will remember their sin no more."

~ Jeremiah 31:34

———◆———

C
an you think of a day when you did not sin? No? How about a moment, just a little moment that was not tainted with sin? No? Me neither.

Sin is so saturated in our world and our lives that we cannot recollect a time when we did not sin. We may think of a time we chose not to sin, or even sins we have worked hard to decrease its influence in our lives and our choice to pursue it. But still, with each waking morning comes a day where we will not even make it an hour without sinning.

For some of us in the church, our past and present sins weigh heavy upon our hearts. It seems so hard to let go of the sin, the memory of sins, of which some of us have such significant sins that they have so changed our lives, our relationships, our futures. It is tough to move on.

Remember this, though, and it is a reminder we need every day. Your sin is paid for. In Christ, your sin has no power over you; it has no control. Christ has destroyed any power sin has over those who are His. As a Christ-follower, God looks at you and sees no sin, just righteousness. To Him, there is not a hint or thought of sin in your life. That is your position before Him; however, the reality is that here we are on this earth, facing a day where we will sin. God knows that sin will continue to be in our lives. We will commit, we will at times pursue it, but there is an ultimate victory from it. Jeremiah writes, "And no longer shall each one teach his neighbor and each his brother, saying, 'Know the Lord' for they shall all know me, from the least of them to the greatest, declares the Lord. For I will forgive their iniquity, and I will remember their sin no more" (Jeremiah 31:34). He is looking ahead to when Christ secures for all time salvation and for an eternity with Christ in Heaven. Jeremiah knows this will be true of him as it is true of you in Christ.

God forgives our sins and remembers them no more!

18

A Call to Return

"I know your works, your toil and your patient endurance, and how
you cannot bear with those who are evil, but have tested those who call
themselves apostles and are not, and found them to be false. I know
you are enduring patiently and bearing up for my name's sake, and
you have not grown weary. But I have this against you, that you have
abandoned the love you had at first. Remember therefore from where
you have fallen; repent and do the works you did at first..."

~ **Revelation 2:2-5b**

———— ◆ ————

When you hold the Bible in your hands, you are holding a book that says it all, from the creation to the return of Christ. Throughout time, the Lord has worked through various ways, people, and organization to bring about His will and demonstrate to the world His grace and love upon all of humanity. Still, even more particularly to those He turns His eyes upon and calls His own. God is presently working and primarily fulfilling His will for the world through His church, understanding though that God works in mysterious ways and will accomplish His purposes in any way He desires. The church always has and will always be a great love of mine as it is a great love of His.

The apostle John wrote Revelation to two particular groups: seven churches specifically existing during the time he was alive, and more generally to the church today. John starts writing to the seven churches in Revelation 2, the first church is in Ephesus. This is the same church Paul wrote to in his letter to the Ephesians. At the start of Revelation 2, John draws out the positives and negatives of this church, providing some stinging criticism out of his great love them, God's people in this church, and for the Lord. Paul spent months with the same church to teach them about Jesus Christ, the Holy Spirit, and how to defeat false teaching. They were off to a great start, eager to learn and live a life of faith in Jesus, a church God would be so proud of. They initially received The Lord's commendations, later His condemnations.

By the time the Lord is writing Revelation and calling out the Ephesians through John, Paul has since been executed in Rome. John is the last of the apostles, witness to the incredible growth, expansion, and strength of the gospel, the church, and the Lord's people. John is wise in addressing both the positives and negatives in the church, just as we now need to wisely analyze the church and her people through the lens of scripture by the hands of the Spirit. The first comments to the Ephesians in Revelation are quite astonishing. He says they toil at their work, they endure life and trials patiently, and cannot stand those who commit evil. They test their leadership to ensure they are of the faith and are not false in their teaching and lives. The church as a whole at this time is under heavy persecution from Rome, and John says they have not grown weary despite the pain of having the government, culture, friends, and family go after them for being Christ-followers. These are all commendable attributes of any church and any church member that we should strive to follow. On the surface, what is not to like about Ephesus? Ephesus initially seems even better than many churches today.

It would seem that at this moment, the Lord could not be happier with Ephesus, but instead of being pleased with them, the Lord is critical of the Ephesians. They are doing everything well, but something is off, something is missing. His indictment on them is one we should all take to heart and consider deeply. The Lord calls the church at Ephesus out, declaring, "But I have this against you, that you have abandoned the love you had at first. Remember therefore from where you have fallen; repent, and do the works you did at first" (Revelation 2:4). God is saying they have forgotten Him. It must have stung their hearts so deeply to be called out in this way not just by a fellow friend and church member, but also by Christ Himself. It is almost like He is saying, "HEY! Remember Me! The One who died for you! The One who loves you! But you left me behind! What were all your works for?" Despite all the amazing things they were doing, they had forgotten the reason why they did all those good things; they forgot their focus and their purpose. They forgot Christ. They had forgotten their passion for Christ, their desire to know Christ, their love for Christ, to live for Christ. You could say the flavor of their faith for Christ had gone, and instead of passionately pursuing Christ, they shrugged their shoulders and moved on from their faith. Their relationship with Christ had merely become a checkmark on the weekend to-do list. Their relationship with Christ had no meaning, no love, no purpose, nothing.

While the Ephesians were cut to their heart over their forgetfulness of Christ and His salvation, we have to reflect on our own relationship with Him and our church as a whole. Reader, you and I are just members of the church, and in the church of Ephesus were members who had not forgotten. Still, John provides us with a caution, a reminder, not to forget Christ and the mighty work He has accomplished in the past: our salvation, those deep and abiding prayers with Him, the suffering He brought that we may seek His glory and will in our lives. His is the greatest love we have ever known, the life-breath of our existence. When the storm is gone, the immediacy of life's troubles is not as large and looming; life becomes more subtle and quiet and settled. Remember, dear Christ-follower, that Christ must always be first in your life, a priority over everything. He deserves nothing less. It is a convicting thought and pray that we, as individual church members and churches, will ask the Lord's critique that we may return to our first love before the completion of time.

It is a hard question to pose to your soul and my soul, but have you lost your first love? Has your storm tempered your heart away from Christ? Are you just doing the motions of being a Christ-follower?

19

God's Glory, Man's Dignity

"What is man that you are mindful of him, and the son of man that you care for him? Yet you have made him a little lower than the heavenly beings and crowned him with glory and honor."

~ Psalm 8:4-5

Growing up in the Los Angeles area night skies in the city and suburban areas typically are lit up with lights, clouding the stars above. I grew up never really knowing what the stars looked like from my home. So rarely do we see the glorious stars shining from galaxies near and far. It's wondrous what Edison's light bulb has allowed us to do all hours of the day and night. What the lightbulb has done though, is to distort the night skies, the stars and galaxies millions of light years away. Think back to the start of creation in Genesis 1:1-5: "In the beginning, God created the heavens and the earth. The earth was without form and void, and darkness was over the face of the deep. And the Spirit of God was hovering over the face of the waters. And God said, 'Let there be light,' and there was light. And God saw that the light was good. And God separated the light from the darkness. God called the light Day, and the darkness he called Night. And there was evening and there was morning, the first day." Living in the light and bright suburbs, we miss out on part of God's creation because we have covered it with our own lights.

But those rare times when I have seen the brilliant night sky, it seems as if the heavens are opened up to put on a majestic show for God's glory. I have yet to see the Northern Lights in person, but can only imagine their dance across the skies of earth, each declaring the splendor and glory of God.

David writes Psalm 8 to display the greatness of God from the heavens down to the earth. Take a moment to read through Psalm 8.

David writes about God's place in the universe and man's place on earth. He says in Psalm 8:1, referring to God, "O Lord, our Lord, how majestic is your name in all the earth! You have set your glory above the heavens." Creation was made in such a way that every part gives glory to God, from the little fly in our house to the beautiful waterfalls in the tropics, from our meager sun to the glories of the heavens. "The heavens declare the glory of God, and the sky above proclaims his handiwork" (Psalm 19:1). All creation declares the glory of God. Everything God does is for His glory, absolutely everything. A humbling thought considering we are the creation, and He is Creator.

Part of God's glory in creating this world, this universe, was to beings who would bring Him glory, by their own choice, their own will. Made in the image of God, humanity was tasked to maintain the earth, to govern the earth, to direct and care for God's creation, all the while giving God the glory due Him. Remember, God's purpose was to declare His glory, and man's purpose was exactly the same, to declare the glory of God. You know the story about man's fall from grace, pursuing personal glory over that of God's. This is still a reality in our present fallen world. Man lost all connection with God, humanity was still to subdue and dominate the earth, but man's dignity had fallen.

In looking up at the stars and contemplating his own existence, David writes in Psalm 8:3-4, "When I look at your heavens, the work of your fingers, the moon and the stars, which you have set in place, what is man that you are mindful of him, and the son of man that you care for him?" David ponders that God is in such a place of majesty, and because of our sin, man lives in his poverty. Why does God still think of humanity?

Throughout the psalms are declarations of God's steadfast love. No matter what humanity has done, God will always think of them. He continues in verse 5-8, "Yet you have made him a little lower than the heavenly beings, and crowned him with glory and honor. You have given him dominion over the works of your hands; you have put all things under his feet, all sheep and oxen and also the beasts of the field, the birds of the heavens, and the fish of the sea, whatever passes along the paths of the sea."

We need to realize God's place and our place in this universe. In this vast universe of ours, even in this minuscule world we live on and in, we think we are in command of so much. If we are honest with ourselves, when we turn our eyes off of ourselves, off of this world, and towards the heavens, what we see is that mankind's place is quite small, yet absolutely significant. Humanity was to subdue the earth, to run and manage it, and in all things bring glory to God.

The Lord has significance for you on this earth, even if you feel your life is not significant. And if you think your life is significant because of you, take a look at the skies and realize that in comparison to the universe, we are absolutely nothing. God has looked upon mankind, placed His image upon them, and in that alone you have a place and a purpose, and anywhere you are, you are a creation of dignity.

David starts and ends Psalm 8, reminding us that our entire existence belongs to the Lord, and because the Lord has touched mankind with dignity, God is worthy of our praise. And when we look to the skies, our hearts, our eyes, our entire beings should turn to the Lord in absolute praise for what He's done.

"O Lord, our Lord, how majestic is your name in all the earth!" (Psalm 8:1)

20

Carried Shame, Transferred Shame

"For I am not ashamed of the gospel, for it is the power of God for salvation to everyone who believes, to the Jew first and also to the Greek. For in it the righteousness of God is revealed from faith for faith, as it is written, 'The righteous shall live by faith.'"

~ **Romans 1:16-17**

Reading through Romans 1, there is no doubt that shame has been carried by sinners, you and I and all of humanity, throughout all of time. Each of us can look back on our lives and see clearly the sins we have committed. We have hurt a fellow brother or sister. We have thought about someone wrongly. The list goes on and on and on into infinity of the sin within humanity's heart. Is some past sin your trial? One that you cannot realize or let go of? The list of sins we could commit and do commit has no end. We look back and see the great shame of our actions - knowing we hurt someone else or took advantage of someone else. We also carry shame when someone calls out our past indiscretions, even when our minds are not aware of it or have long forgotten our unrepented sin. You may have confessed, sought forgiveness and reconciliation in this life and in Christ it is granted to you. Still, as we know and can see, sin has consequences, and while we are on this earth, absent from the presence of Christ, we will face the consequences of our sin and others' sin until we are in the presence of Christ. Sin and its consequences affect all on earth, the saved and unsaved.

We should be ashamed of our sins. It is ours; we did it, we must own it and confess our sin before the Lord, seeking repentance. We are ashamed of what we have done in the past, but let me ask you, are you ashamed of Christ? Are you ashamed of the gospel? Are you ashamed of your calling to believe in Christ as your Lord and Savior? In this increasingly hostile world, are you ashamed of the one thing that can save a soul from separation from God and eternal torment? These questions are to consider, dwell upon, and are not to be taken lightly.

The one thing this world hates is Christ. You watch the news and social media, and it is all over the place. You listen to conversations across the country, and there is a blanket rejection of Christ and the gospel. You can talk about "god" all you want, but the moment you say Jesus' name, the conversation stalls, gets quiet, ends, or is even hostile. Are we ashamed of Christ? Are we ashamed to have mentioned His name? Are we ashamed because of the fear of man?

In his first chapter to the Romans, Paul calls out every inconceivable sin of his day, truly our day also. To the world, those sins are no big deal, and what surprises us today did not surprise Paul 2,000 years ago. This world is sinful and immersed, embedded, controlled by our own selfish ambition and our pursuit of sin.

But here in Romans 1, Paul makes an obvious separation from the world, listing shameful things, declaring all sin as shameful. And then in verses 16-17, Paul writes, "For I am not ashamed of the gospel, for it is the power of God for salvation to everyone who believes, to the Jew first and also to the Greek. For in it the righteousness of God is revealed from faith for faith, as it is written, 'The righteous shall live by faith,'" exclaiming the one thing we should not be ashamed of, the gospel of Christ and him crucified. At the start of this small but powerful passage, Paul declares, "For I am not ashamed."

As Paul started writing Romans, he looked back over his own life, just as you did at the start of this passage. He thinks of all the sins he has participated in and seen throughout his life. He most likely considers the persecution and executions of Christians he instigated, promoted, and sanctioned before his salvation in

Christ. I am sure that Paul reflected on the faces of those believers he targeted so many years ago, the living and the dead, targeted by him because of Christ. That is the story of Saul, dark and shameful, before Christ intervened and changed his name to Paul. That is the story of the world. That is my story and your story before Christ.

Here, though, Paul calls out to believers that their shame is no longer theirs. Those deeds, those sins, those thoughts all done in sinful flesh are gone. What do you have to stand on now that Christ has taken your shame away? You no longer stand on your shame, you stand on the gospel of Christ, the salvation of Christ, that He may remove from your back the shame dragging down the gospel in our lives because we are holding onto our share of past sin.

Why and how can Paul so willingly remove his baggage of shame? He can do it because he knows the Man who can do it. His name is Jesus Christ. Paul does not carry his shame anymore because of the goodness and sacrifice of Christ. He says regarding the gospel, "for it is the power of God for salvation to everyone who believes."

Paul gladly and unashamedly carries the gospel of Christ throughout the Roman Empire until his execution in Rome, not for killing Christians, but for being a Christian.

You and I so often carry our shame, secretly and quietly, not re-alizing that it hinders our ability to share the gospel and salvation in Christ to a hostile world that so desperately needs Christ and the truth and beauty of salvation in Christ. Will you lay this bur-den of past sin at the foot of the cross and pray for the delightful burden of being in Christ as Christ declares in Matthew 11:28-30, "Come to me, all who labor and are heavy laden, and I will give you rest. Take my yoke upon you, and learn from me, for I am gentle and lowly in heart, and you will find rest for your souls. For my yoke is easy, and my burden is light."?

Will you lay any fears of declaring Christ before a hostile world before His feet? Let Him carry the world and all its past, present, and future shame, as He lets you carry the gospel to the world's end.

21

Hurt Yet Healed

"Behold, blessed is the one whom God reproves; therefore, despise not the discipline of the Almighty. For he wounds, but binds up; he shatters, but his hands heal."

~ Job 5:17-18

———◆———

Have you looked at your trial, your suffering, and said, "That was good"? Not good in the sense that it was enjoyable, not good in that you hurt so very badly, not good in the sense of losing over winning, but good in that at the end of it all, you see the benefit in it. It may take a while, but at some point, in this journey out of the storm, I pray that you will see the goodness of suffering, pain, and loss in your life. I pray you find goodness in the outcome, goodness in who you were and who you are becoming. Job says those that God has brought through difficult times are blessed: "Behold, blessed is the one whom God reproves; therefore, despise not the discipline of the Almighty. For he wounds, but binds up; he shatters, but his hands heal." It is astounding to look at life and say that trials are a good thing. For a moment after reading this verse, I imagined being a friend of Job and giving him a quizzical look, like, "Are you crazy, Job? You just lost everything, bro, and you say that you are one blessed by God?" Take a moment and look over your trial; what blessings did you see, big or small? What blessings were present either during the trial or you see now after the trial?

During my brain cancer diagnosis, surgeries, and treatments, my family kept a book of blessings, things the Lord had done, prayers that were answered. It was a joy to see God's handiwork in my life during that time, directing each little thing that needed to be completed. As I recovered in 2015 primarily from the cranial radiation, and as I wrote *Anchored in the Storm*, I began to realize that this major trial and suffering of my life was an absolute blessing. I would even call it the greatest gift I have ever received, after salvation through Christ of course. I would not trade that time, that suffering for anything; absolutely nothing could replace the great joy of this time in my life. It set my life on a better course than I ever imagined for myself. Was it an easy road? Absolutely not! But it was an absolute joy to trust the Lord's work in my life, to see the Spirit call me and those walking with me during that time to a stronger faith. And most of all, I was able to write about the Lord to you. I consider myself so very blessed to be writing to you, dear reader.

It is hard in any part of life to take on something more difficult than we would like. We want an easy life, a comfortable life, an enjoyable life, but God does something wondrous in times of difficulty and pain. He calls us for a time, to walk closely and intimately with Him, to depend and trust in Him that His will be done for His glory. He wants more of our hearts and will work so that He plays a bigger role in our lives than even we play in our own lives. Job understands that these types of situations in our lives are meant to turn us to the Lord. From dawn to dusk, from birth to death, our lives on this earth as Christ-followers are for Him, for His purpose.

Yes, God challenges us or allows us to be hurt, but remember that in challenging us, God also heals. There is purpose in the hurt and great blessing in the healing. Christian suffering is not purposeless: it all has meaning and purpose directed by the Lord. He wants to accomplish something in your life, and in order to accomplish that He needs to refine our lives and take us out into storms where we are challenged and tested. The author of Hebrews reiterates Job in Hebrews 12:6a: "For the Lord disciplines the one he loves." It is a strange way to show love, but God is working in your life to make you more like Himself, and discipline is one of the many ways God works.

God gave you a time of discipline and as you come out of that time, consider the Lord's gift in your time of healing. It's strange to think that God allows hurt in our lives, but the allowance is out of His love and grace, and the healing is also out of His love and grace. God loved you from the beginning of time, and He loved you as you were when He called you to salvation, but God, as a great and loving Father, does not want you to remain as you are; He wants you to be better. Both the suffering and healing are out of love, for your good, that you may become a better person, a person made in the likeness of Him, Christlike in every way. It's a strange thing for our hearts and minds to understand that His mighty love for you causes hurt, but in that hurt, that great hurt you have just been through, comes His healing. You will also find the magnificent love He has for you. His goal is not to make you bitter, but better!

One thing we must remember about God is that things happen in His timing, and as you heal, you'll find that it may take longer than you think. There may be a day when the doctor says you are cancer-free, a time when the bank account shows a positive balance, when a company calls to offer a job or when that broken relationship is restored. Healing tends to take much longer than we are expecting in our instant world, but be patient in healing. It takes time.

I remember thinking once I had finished radiation and chemo that life would return to the way it was, that my health would return to the way it was, that life would be the same. However, here I am six years later and what I am realizing is that healing is still happening, the shock of cancer has worn off, but the shadow of cancer remains in each doctor's appointment, each little health issue, even each little headache. In each moment I recall my cancer and that journey. That does not mean I have not physically recovered, but this new life requires a new understanding of what life meant. Healing brings new realities to our lives out of the storm, but it also brings great hope and love of God. As Job reminds us, what God has broken, He will also repair. Unlike His hands in creation, instantly creating everything you see, He desires to take His hands and delicately mold and shape the life you live as a fine masterpiece of His beloved child.

22

Supposed to Be

"And all these, though commended through their faith, did not receive what was promised, since God had provided something better for us, that apart from us they should not be made perfect."

~ Hebrews 11: 39-40

———•◆•———

As a kid, what hopes and dreams did you have about your future, your career, your marriage, your home, your travels? So many dreams lay ahead in your youth. The dreams of a child are almost limitless. How about now that you are an adult? What was your life supposed to be like? As you look back on your life, what dreams and desires for the future have happened? As you look presently, what dreams and desires are undone and are no longer a possibility? How is life working out for you?

I look back on my own dreams growing up and remember my fond expectations of what was to come. It was supposed to be a great life. I look back and see a big chasm between what I dreamt and what is now a reality in my late thirties. Life looks completely different from what I imagined and as I reflect on the past, I realize that today I have a life I never wanted. Maybe a better wording of that is a life I never expected. Life is not what it was supposed to be. If we are honest with ourselves, we can all understand that the dreams we had for the future are not the outcomes of our reality.

Think back over the entirety of the Bible, from Genesis to Revelation. Think about the challenges faced by many of the people in the Bible. What might they have imagined their lives were going to be like? Adam and Eve were supposed to stay in the Garden of Eden working to cultivate and grow this lush garden paradise. Even more than that, they walked with God and talked with God, conversing personally with Him. They were supposed to be in the Garden, but they were forced out because of their sin. Abraham was supposed to stay in Ur raising his family and growing his herds but God called him to leave Ur and head to an unknown land. Joseph was supposed to stay with his brothers and family, expanding their families and herds, but ended up tied up by his brothers and sold into slavery. Moses was supposed to be one in the upper echelon of Egyptian leadership, maybe even Pharaoh himself, not a shepherd in the Sinai raising someone else's sheep having lost all ties to the Egyptian royal family. David was supposed to be a shepherd, a man after God's own heart, a king of Israel, not an adulterer, a murderer, leaving a legacy of anarchy, chaos, and ultimately the fall of his family and monarchy in Israel. Solomon was supposed to be the wisest man the world had ever seen, but pursued women, wealth, and military power against the command of the Lord to literally waste this vapor of life. Peter was supposed to be a fisherman on the Sea of Galilee, not a denier of the Messiah he had come to follow and adore.

We were all supposed to be something, but somehow, we got in the way with our personal sin, and we split with God. Our lives as we supposed it to be would ever be tainted between what could be and what is. Some of those "supposed to be" of our lives become the "never will" of our present reality. Yet, God, through His mercy and grace, takes our lives as Christ-followers and moves them into a life that we never imagined.

Rather than our own sinful actions, sometimes our "supposed to be" is changed by the hand of God wanting to take us another direction. Our lives are a mix of God's gracious reckoning and refinement into becoming a more Christlike person. An honest assessment of the ups and downs of our lives will reveal that the "supposed to be" formed in the past became the "never will" of our present realities. We can live mourning a life we never expected, but what kind of life is that? As Christ-followers, we can move onto a life of the never imagined.

And that is where you and I are today after the difficulties and storms we faced in our past. We exit the storm to a place that never crossed our mind, a place our dreams never went. We have the option to hold onto those dreams that never were and never will be, fictions we wanted for ourselves. Or we can embrace the reality of God's sovereign hand in our lives, allowing and shaping certain parts to make us into His greater likeness and beauty. We could look at the life that is and embrace the wonder that God is actively working in our lives, ever-present as we navigate the shifting waters of life.

I never expected brain cancer at the age of 32. Actually, I never expected any type of cancer and knew nothing about brain cancer. But as I reflect on how these past few years have gone, I realize that most of my "supposed to be" are now "never will." I realize the goodness and kindness of the Lord in my life as He sovereignly directed each step, each turn, each wave and storm of my life. If you were to ask me if I would ever want to give up my cancer, and the varying difficulties of this life for the life I dreamed for myself, I would emphatically exclaim "NO!" I could not trade the world for my cancer. Aside from salvation, my cancer was the greatest gift I have ever received, and I have no qualms about saying that. How would you choose if you could receive the world over your suffering? If we were to look back over the men and women of the Old and New Testaments, would they trade their suffering and the lessons learned?

Jesus is the only person whose life went exactly as planned. From His birth to His teaching in the Temple at 12, to His entry on the scene declaring Himself Messiah, to His healing and feeding thousands, to His death and resurrection and ascension to Heaven. Jesus knew exactly what life was going to be like. As with any human, He looked for a different path in the Garden of Gethsemane, yet as God, He knew the cross was the only way to save humanity from their sins and eternity in Hell.

The glory for Jesus, through all the pain and suffering, was that humanity could be saved through faith in Him as Lord and Savior. Hope lay with and in Him and no matter what you thought life was "supposed to be," God has orchestrated and allowed certain things to happen for His glory and your benefit. The life you live in Christ, no matter the valleys and mountain peaks, is the exact life you are supposed to live. As a kid, you probably did not imagine a relationship with God Almighty and here you are a Christ-follower carefully directed and formed by the very hands of God.

The "never imagined" life you are presently living with Christ by your side is far more beautiful than the life that was "supposed to be."

23

Before God All the Same

"The rich and the poor meet together, the Lord is the maker of them all."

~ **Proverbs 22:2**

———◆———

I am not an overly competitive person. I have always thought that I am my toughest competitor. If you are like me, you also realize that competition is out there. In the 21st century, truly every aspect of our lives is a competition.

Does your family look like this other family? Do your kids act like those other kids? Is your salary as high as the family sitting three rows ahead of you? Was your trip as exciting and enthralling as those people walking by? Are you busy or busier than your coworkers? Are you holier than those sitting in the pew next to you? It is an endless cycle of comparison and competition. Social media is as much of a problem in the church as it is outside the church. And while we peruse social media profiles and accounts, we are comparing ourselves to others and competing with them. It is a natural, though not healthy, addiction we all have, even if we think we do not.

Equality is a constant topic of conversation today. We hear about it all over the place, in the media, political movements, and schools to name a few. Of course, we would love to live in a world where we all have equal standing wherever we go, but we live in a fallen world, and as long as we live in a fallen world, we will always be unequal in position, in finances, in family, in beauty, in strength, in possessions, in all of life. That sounds a bit depressing, but in the presence of Christ, before the throne of God, every man, every woman stands equal. God does not look at us and evaluate us based on our height, our weight, our looks, our wealth or our poverty. He looks at us as His creation, people created in His image. Even though we are a fallen creation, He shows us that what He has made is good, is worthy, is equal. We do not need to compare because what we see and want to be does not matter to Him; what matters is a heart turned towards Him.

In "To the Reader" at the start of *Anchored to the Son*, I gave an example of coming out of a storm, back to the calm of daily life. Imagine once again you are standing on the beach after the storm. You look around and see families enjoying the beautiful beach weather. You see couples sitting there contemplating their futures, reflecting on their past. You see carefree moments, but is life meant to be carefree? As you stand there breathing in the sea air for the first time in a long time, relishing the moment of knowing the storm has ended, wiggling your toes in the warm sand, you realize that there is something more to life than what you thought. Life does not get any better or any worse if your grass is a little brown, or if your trip to the campground was not as thrilling as your neighbor's trip to Tahiti, or if your bank account is a little less or significantly less than that family at church because God does not look at those things. At no point will God ask to look at your bank account, but at all points, He will ask to look at your heart.

God's perspective on humanity is revealed in 1 Samuel 16, as Samuel is tasked with anointing the next king of Israel. He was previewing all of David's brothers looking at their strength, their build, their commanding presence. God reminds Samuel in verse 7, "Do not look on his appearance or on the height of his stature, because I have rejected him. For the Lord sees not as man sees; man looks on the outward appearance, but the Lord looks on the heart."

You have been given a great gift as you walk onto the beach from the storm of your trial. The Lord has allowed it partially to help you understand that all humanity is His. God wants us to see His creation as He does. Instead of evaluating and judging, we should reach out and care for them. The great kindness of the Lord is that He took His hands and molded part of you to do life according to His way, not by the world's ways and standards. God's ways are always in contrast to the world's. How you look at another must be different. It is going to be a struggle to look at someone, no matter their situation, as a creation of the Lord God Almighty, but He is challenging each of us to do so. We are not called to look at others as we want to see them, but as He sees them. And if they are lost souls then we proclaim the gospel, and should the graciousness of the Lord prevail, they will be saved.

"The Lord is the maker of [us] all!"

24

A Place Prepared

"Let not your heart be troubled. Believe in God, believe also in me. In my Father's house are many rooms. If it were not so, would I have told you that I go to prepare a place for you? And if I go to prepare a place for you, I will come again and will take you to myself, that where I am you may be also. And you know the way to where I am going."

~ John 14:1-4

————— ♦ —————

No matter how adventurous we are or how close to home we like to stay, we can all agree that after any vacation, no matter how good it was, it is always nice to be home. As people, we like to have a place to call our own, a place of refuge, a place fitting who we are. No matter how big or small, clean or cluttered, whether it is the home we want or not, it is home. There is some comfort after being gone for a while, a great joy in our hearts knowing that we are home. Have you ever felt that there is more to the idea of "home" than we understand here on earth?

Jesus and the disciples are talking about "home" in John 14. It is the last night of Jesus' life on the earth. In His mind dwells His impending death, but He prioritizes and cherishes these last few moments He has with these men. During these last hours, there are a variety of questions, answers and discussions throughout the gospels between Jesus and the disciples. Jesus senses their troubled souls. They had devoted three years of their lives to Him and now it all seems to be falling apart, along with everything they had anticipated that Jesus would do. Jesus senses their struggle with what is coming and wants to provide them comfort. They know He is leaving this earth, but Jesus wants to communicate to them that in Him life is just starting, and home is not here.

He starts the conversation, "Let not your hearts be troubled." I do not know the sound of Jesus' voice, but imagine the most soothing voice saying, "Do not worry." His voice is one of comfort and hope, despite what He will face in the coming hours, including crucifixion. He brings comfort to them, the comfort of "home." He says, "In my Father's house are many rooms." If Buckingham Palace has 775 rooms, Windsor Castle has around 1,000 (too many rooms to count!), and the White House has a paltry 132, just imagine the number of rooms in the house of the Lord, a place for each of His children. We do not know how many people will have a room in the house of the Lord, but Buckingham Palace has nothing on that place.

Jesus reassures the disciples with the comfort of home, and reminds them there will be a day when they will all be together in the same house, taken care of by the Lord, forever. They struggle to realize the implications that Jesus must leave them, but in leaving them. They don't understand that Jesus is going to work for them. When each is called by the Lord to come home, to be with Him in Heaven, each will realize the full meaning of this short, but deep conversation.

As Jesus is preparing a place for the disciples, so He is preparing (has prepared) a place for His many children throughout the centuries—a place called home. It is not a place on land owned by Jesus, like a caretaker's cottage at Windsor Castle; it is a place inside Jesus home, a place He has prepared specifically for you. This isn't like a huge hotel that is nice, but extremely generic. It's not a place with room numbers, but a place specifically handcrafted for you, with your name on the door, a place of love and comfort, a gift from the Savior Himself. He doesn't just want to save you and then move on. He does not just want to exist with you; He wants to live with you. He wants to know you deeply and intimately, to the depth of your soul. He wants to be a part of your life and you to be a part of His. It is a miraculous thought, but my mind struggles to comprehend this place created by Him. And that is just a part of what He is creating for those who are called by His name, sealed with His Spirit. The thoughts silence and astound us.

You may have struggled at home growing up; it may not have been a loving home. It may have been a home where the struggles were clear and defined, or a home where everything looked perfect, but the secrets and dysfunctions were carefully hidden away. It may have been a home of great poverty and hunger, a home seemingly abandoned by society itself. Or it may have been a very lovely, loving home filled with the Lord. Whatever our background with the concept of "home" on this earth, nothing is going to compare to the reality of "home" forever, eternal, with the Lord Almighty. And when the Lord calls us home, as He will each of His disciples, then and only then, will we truly be home!

No matter how hard home has been for you here in this sin-soaked world, have hope because Jesus has not just a home, but a room for you in His home. And what better home can there be either on earth or in heaven, than in Jesus' home. It's real and it's there. Jesus has prepared it to greet you into His presence. Go forward knowing there is a secure place for you!

25

Produces ... Produces ... Produces

"Not only that, we rejoice in our sufferings, knowing that suffering produces endurance, and endurance produces character, and character produces hope, and hope does not put us to shame, because God's love has been poured into our hearts through the Holy Spirit who has been given to us."

~ Romans 5:3-5

———◆———

Paul has a most wondrous look at life: "We rejoice in our sufferings." Were you able to rejoice in your suffering? Assuming at this point that the suffering is over for you, can you look back and rejoice with the Lord in the sufferings you experienced? It is a difficult question to answer, requiring much time, thought, and reflection, which is not the easiest of tasks. Take a moment and review your suffering. God allowed suffering for you. Jesus Himself says, in Matthew 7:11, "If you then, who are evil, know how to give good gifts to your children, how much more will your Father who is in heaven give good things to those who ask him!" Can you affirm that your suffering from God was good?

It is going to sound odd, but this gift of suffering, and now healing and recovery, was a gift of love. God loves you so much that He allowed suffering in your life. It is so inconsistent with the gifts we give as people, but God gives us suffering for a variety of reasons: to draw us closer to Him, to take our eyes off this world and place them onto Him, to trust Him for His provision during those dark days, and to refine us and make us more like Him. He wants to produce a variety of things. Paul declares in Romans 5:1-5: "Therefore, since we have been justified by faith, we have peace with God through our Lord Jesus Christ. Through him we have also obtained access by faith into this grace in which we stand, and we rejoice in hope of the glory of God. Not only that, we rejoice in our sufferings, knowing that suffering produces endurance, and endurance produces character, and character produces hope, and hope does not put us to shame, because God's love has been poured into our hearts through the Holy Spirit who has been given to us."

Think for a moment about the amazing road you have ahead out of the storm and all the things you are going to produce in your life by the hand of the Holy Spirit. It is a wondrous list that Paul gives us: suffering gives us endurance, endurance brings forth a refined and deeper character, and deep within our souls hope arises knowing God is going to act now and in the future just as He acted in the past. Perhaps the most stunning thing in Paul's list is that God has poured His love into our hearts. God has declared your name and through His Spirit has delivered this great out-pouring of His love into your soul.

As the calm returns to your life, consider all those traits the Lord has worked on and honed in your life and go forth in His great love to help others produce those same traits.

26

No Depth, No Root, No Gain

"And other seeds fell into good soil and produced grain, growing up and increasing and yielding thirtyfold and sixtyfold and a hundredfold. And he said, 'He who has ears to hear, let him hear.'"

~ Mark 4:8-9

———— ♦ ————

Throughout the gospels, Jesus has a wonderful way of using parables or stories to illustrate a point. One reality of parables is that Jesus told them for those who would believe in Him, not necessarily for those who do not believe. In Mark 4:1-20, Jesus is going to tell a story about a farmer planting a crop in preparation for the harvest and the fruit of his planting. In today's world, most of us do not know how to grow food, process food, and even provide food for ourselves outside a grocery store or a restaurant. It is the nature of our time, but even just a century ago, most people knew how to grow food and would relate closely to Jesus' parable. Today in the 21st century, it's a little bit harder to relate.

The story starts with a farmer in Judea. Spring has arrived and if he does not get his seeds sown and planted, there will be no harvest and no food for survival or profit. The farmer plants his crop using traditional means, taking a handful of seeds and throwing them onto the field. This process had been used for thousands of years and really did not change until the Agricultural Revolution in the 18th century. The farmer scatters his seed anywhere on his land, hoping for a good crop. The seed is distributed onto the path, rocky ground, among the thorns, and good soil.

First, we must look at the farmer, the sower of the seeds. Who is he? He spreads seeds, throwing it about as he goes about his life. In a way, Christ is the farmer. As He is living His life on this earth, He shares the truth of who He is, the reasons He came to earth, and the salvation He brings not just for Israel, but all people, Jews and Gentiles alike. In another way, you and I are the farmer. As we go about our day sharing Christ with the people we encounter. As the calm comes into your life, you have a story to tell of Christ's redemption and the Spirit's work in your suffering and the purposes you have learned. As a Christ-follower, many wonder how your life is different and how you have gone through the storms the way you have. Small comments about your faith, perseverance, and strength allow you to extend that conversation into a gospel conversation. A sower is one who spreads seeds, and as previously stated, back in the day the seeds went everywhere. Today as we sow the Word, it is not our job to pick and choose who to share the gospel with because at the end of the day, remember that all of us are unworthy of the gospel. One of God's precious children, and possibly many, shared the gospel with you, who were unworthy of the gospel. The Lord will do His work when the seed is planted, and remember, the harvest is all in His time.

Jesus has a story about each type of ground the seeds were distributed on, a story for each of us to think and consider as we look at our faith, our hearts, the life ahead, and the life we want out of the storm.

The first soil the seeds hit was the path. The path may have gone from one field to the next, hard and compact from all the people using it, existing for years. The farmer passes by as he is sowing his seed. The seed lands on the path, and there it sits and sits until the birds come along to enjoy a free meal given by the farmer. Jesus says that those that fall on the path hear the Word: "when they hear, Satan immediately comes and takes away the word that is sown in them" (Mark 4:15). The seed is quickly taken without any growth, even any chance of growth. It is heard and immediately forgotten, in one ear and out the other.

The second soil the seeds hit was the rocks: "It did not have much soil, and immediately it sprang up, since it had no depth of soil." It grew quickly, possibly like you, initially interested in Christ, but the reality is that when challenges came and the world called, the growth could not be sustained. It is a sad state when you see someone come to the Lord with passion for Christ and His church and then they walk away. Regular life calls, or possibly even a trial at the outset, and slowly any sign of passion for Christ is gone. It truly is sad within our churches, and I will say that I am sure all of us can do a better job of coming alongside each other and helping others grow in their relationship with Christ and making sure that growth in Christ is sustained and permanent.

The third soil Jesus spoke of was among thorns. The seed was thrown, but choked by the thorns. Though the seed grew into a plant, the thorns would not allow it to fully grow and choked it off without any opportunity for growing any fruit. It is very similar to the seeds thrown on the rocks. There was some life, some growth, but it was cut off. Again, another sad state for what initially appeared to be a fervent faith.

The last soil was the field itself. It had "good soil, and produced grain, growing up and increasing and yielding thirtyfold and sixtyfold and a hundredfold" (verse 8). The farmer is much pleased with the seed thrown here. In its time, the seeds grow to plants, and then the harvest, the collection of all the fruit. I love that Jesus says, "thirtyfold ... sixtyfold ... hundredfold." He is saying that our sowing and planting will present differences between us, some Christ-followers will produce more and others less, but the key is not how much is produced, but that some are produced and that we are faithful in sharing and planting the gospel. If the seed just stayed in a sack, there would be no harvest, nothing for the farmer to display at the market, no benefit.

Above all, in this earth and in the church, we are called to spread the seeds of the gospel. Sometimes we will see a harvest, someone coming to faith in Jesus Christ as Lord and Savior. Like your past, there was someone who planted a seed in your life, and you were given an incredible opportunity to see that seed grow to fruition, but remember the harvest is up to the work of Christ, and we have the work of spreading seeds. God is going to use us to spread the gospel to the world.

The question we must ask ourselves, of course, is which soil are we? The soil is our heart, so what is the condition of our heart? How is our heart doing? Are we in a place where we can confidently and boldly share the gospel, letting the gospel grow in a person's life as the Lord wills?

Your story is how God has worked and is working in your life; sow the seed of the gospel wherever you go!

27

Who is This?

"Go and tell John what you have seen and heard: the blind receive their sight, the lame walk, lepers are cleansed, and the deaf hear, the dead are raised up, the poor have good news preached to them."

~ Luke 7:22

From birth, John the Baptist had a unique role in the annals of biblical history. For four hundred years since the book of Malachi was written, there was no word from God, no prophet from God, just utter silence. The Romans had since conquered Israel and cut a deal with the Jewish religious leaders: the Romans and the Jews all got power, although it was an extremely tenuous relationship. Four hundred years of silence and then we hear about the coming of John the Baptist in Luke 1:3-24. There will be a miraculous birth for the aged Elizabeth and Zechariah, faithful servants of the Lord and distant relations to Mary, the mother of Jesus. Luke writes about John's coming and future career as a prophet in the wilderness in Luke 1:17: "and he will go before him [meaning John the Baptist] in the spirit and power of Elijah, to turn the hearts of fathers to the children, and the disobedient to the wisdom of the just, to make ready for the Lord a people prepared."

John is born and goes forth among the people of Israel declaring, "Repent, for the kingdom of heaven is at hand.' For this is he who was spoken of by the prophet Isaiah when he said, 'The voice of one crying in the wilderness; 'Prepare the way of the Lord; make his paths straight'" (Matthew 3:2-3). John devotes his life and his reputation, going against the grain of Jewish and Roman culture, to declare the coming of the Messiah, a man whom God promised would come from the dawn of time in Genesis 3.

By the time the Messiah comes on the scene ready to declare and show His nature as God to the people of Israel, to the Roman Empire, and to the entire world, John the Baptist has been at work for years fulfilling Isaiah's prophecy in Isaiah 40:3: "A voice cries; 'In the wilderness prepare the way of the Lord; make straight in the desert a highway of our God." John is like a town crier who goes forth to say the King is coming; salvation is at hand. He declares to all, "Make way for the King!" John preached and baptized people, becoming an odd celebrity in his camel's hair clothing and food of honey and locusts, drawing even Jewish religious leaders to follow him among other genuine followers.

Rumblings came out to the wilderness of Israel, where John was baptizing a man who was remarkably, seemingly and miraculously healing people. John knew he was destined to "prepare the way of the Lord," but in no way did he have the power to heal and do the works of this person he hears about. He and his followers have conversations and discussions on what is happening and who is doing these wonderous things. They sit around the fire all pondering, "Who is this?" Not sure who this miracle worker is; John sends two of his followers to investigate this person and the rumored healings.

After hours, if not days, of traveling the dusty roads, John's followers approach this man who is talking to and working with a rather large crowd. John's disciples ask the man they came to see, "Are you the one who is to come, or shall we look for another?" (Luke 7:19). As the two are questioning the man, the miracle worker goes to work healing many people. They watch this man working, but are still wondering, "Who is this man?" The man is healing in front of the whole crowd, and suddenly he turns his head towards John's followers and says, "Go and tell John what you have seen and heard: the blind receive their sight, the lame walk, lepers are cleansed, and the deaf hear, the dead are raised up, the poor have good news preached to them. And blessed is the one who is not offended by me" (Luke 7:22-23). Jesus' eyes pierce the two men while He declares this incredible statement. It was not just the statement that astounded them, but it is also the phrase that gets lost in the wonders of Jesus' work. Jesus says, "Go and tell John what you have seen." It was not just the stories they heard of these miracles, but two things they saw: Jesus heal and Jesus Himself, confirming who He is. They were first-hand witnesses to the works of Jesus in the lives of probably dozens who were sick and now healed by the hands of Jesus. The question for these two disciples of John is no longer "Who is this?" because there is no longer a question to be asked. They know who Jesus is. Their questions, their thoughts, their suspicions had all been answered in what they heard and what they saw. They return to where John was working in the wilderness and report to him, who later baptizes Jesus and declares, "And I have seen and have borne witness that this is the Son of God" (John 1:34).

Those healed by Jesus, John the Baptist, and his followers all declare the work of Jesus in their lives, and Jesus affirms their witness. And those witnesses all declare who Jesus is wherever they go. Each has been changed in a variety of ways as they interacted with Jesus; they know who He is!

Now, here you are, the chaos of the trials you have endured is turning towards healing, so you have your own "Who is this?" meeting with Jesus. As you reflect on your recent suffering, what did Jesus do in your life? How was your life changed by the presence of the Spirit? Lastly, what are you going to say about this man who everyone is talking about? Who is He? Take some time to consider and pray what your life and testimony say about Jesus and what you would proclaim about Jesus.

You have been given an opportunity out of your storm to declare the goodness and work of Christ in your life. While I was in my storm, I wrote down quotes, sayings, songs, and verses that stood out to me and encouraged me. These things showed me the Lord and His work in a new light, a light in the darkness through suffering, a light unfiltered by this world. While I recovered from cranial radiation and chemotherapy in 2015, I started to write, to put those quotes, sayings, songs, and verses into a declaration of what Christ did in my own chaos and storm. Initially, I wrote more for my own soul, but then God inspired me that someone else may benefit from the words I was writing of Christ's work in my life. It gave me a chance to declare to the world through writing. Out of your own storm, you have such an incredible testimony to declare to a world that is looking for hope, a hope that can only be found in Christ. You are like John and his followers, "who have seen and have borne witness that this is the Son of God" (John 1:34).

The world is seeking hope, freedom, and salvation, but is looking everywhere to everything, except to Christ. Now is the time to tell your story, your witness to the power and work of Jesus Christ in your life. It may be speaking at your church, starting a blog, writing a book, mentoring believers. The work you have ahead is absolutely limitless because you serve a Savior who is limitless!

28

F.A.T.

"God is faithful, by whom you were called into the fellowship of his Son, Jesus Christ our Lord."

~ 1 Corinthians 1:9

When I was in college, oh so many years ago, I knew the Lord was leading me to leave the church I grew up in to serve Him at another church. The congregation I was leaving was one I attended for 20 years, the church where I met the Lord, committed my life to Him, and was saved. It was the church with an amazing group of people I loved, including my parents who were staying at the church. It is always hard to leave a place you love, especially if not everyone understands the need to leave such a good church. But when the Lord calls, you answer. It was several years of praying for the church the Lord would want me to be in, quietly conversing with others about their church, what they liked, what they did not like, even asking advice of those I trusted on whether I should be leaving a church at all, and even some very difficult conversations with those who did not take the time to consider God's call on my heart. There was a moment when my prayers were answered.

My mentor and friend, Steve Stark, and I had just met for dinner. At the end of our conversation outside my apartment, he told me that he and Todd Smith, who would be the pastor, were starting a church. At that moment, I knew the Lord had answered my prayer of where I should go. I knew Steve, I did not know Todd at the time, but beyond that, I knew the Lord was in this and calling me to this church, to Crossroads Community Church.

Todd and I met officially a bit later for the first time over coffee to talk about the church, why the Lord was calling him to start a church, how he was going to do it, and the role I might play as someone committed to the Lord's work in this faithful quest. He was very sure about who he felt would be good candidates to join the launch team, the group of people to get the church off the ground. He said he was looking for F.A.T. people. It took me aback initially, but then he explained the type of people the universal church needed: Faithful, Available, and Teachable - F.A.T. I wasn't insulted at all. These are the type of people the Lord was looking for throughout the Bible, not a perfect people, but a committed people.

Faithful

Where does one start with the idea of a faithful Christian? Does the word "faithful" mean loyal? Steady? True? Devoted? Reliable? Trusted? Any one of those words, if not all, describe the word "faithful."

One starts looking at a faithful Christian by looking at a faithful God, the supreme example of faithfulness. Throughout the Psalms, we see God's faithfulness declared across its pages. The author of Psalm 33 writes of God's faithfulness in verse 4: "For the word of the Lord is upright, and all his works are done in faithfulness." The Lord works faithfully for the sake of His people, day in, day out. He is asking for the same faithfulness, not that we can work day in and day out without needing a rest. Still, despite our circumstances, the good and the bad, we never tire of a relationship with Him, of becoming more and more like Him, of sharing His salvation with those we come in contact with.

In being faithful, we know that God is always ours, and we are always His.

Available

The Lord is going to work as the Lord is going to work. Sometimes our plans fit with how He is going to work; other times, our plans do not align with His plans. The Lord is asking us to be available for His call to ministry, His plan.

When I was praying and considering a new church I had to be available for God's call. We have to be available just as He called us into our trials, and thus the ministry we have when the trials end. The work of the Spirit is always in His timing, and He will use a plethora of circumstances to bring that about. We just need to be available for this work.

Consider Isaiah, the Old Testament prophet, for a moment. He was a man fully consecrated and eager to do the Lord's work. The Lord had granted Isaiah an extraordinary experience in allowing him to see Heavens' glories, and above all God, Himself. We see this vision in Isaiah 6:3 with seraphim (angels) flying around, all praising the Lord, "Holy, holy, holy is the Lord of hosts; the whole earth is full of his glory!" Isaiah soon realizes his own inabilities before God, declaring before the throne of God, "Woe is me! For I am lost; for I am a man of unclean lips, and I dwell in the midst of a people of unclean lips; for my eyes have seen the King, the LORD of hosts!" (Isaiah 6:5).

Isaiah felt utterly inadequate to receive the unspeakable vision he was gifted, but he knew the Lord would use this for a plan and a purpose. Isaiah was ready for the moment God would call. In verse 8, the Lord makes that call upon Isaiah: "And I heard the voice of the Lord saying, 'Whom shall I send, and who will go for us?'" (Isaiah 6:8). Barely a second and heartbeat later, Isaiah replies, "Here am I! Send me." The astounding thing is that Isaiah doesn't even know what the Lord is asking him to do. You see, Isaiah is not waiting for a particular opportunity to work for the Lord. The particular opportunity is working for the Lord. He does not tell God of his talents and skills, or the talents and skills he doesn't have. He doesn't tell God the things he enjoys and the things he does not enjoy. The Lord calls, and Isaiah answers, and in Isaiah's mind, "That is that!" He moves into the Lord's will wherever the Lord will take him.

We did not have the talents and skills needed to get through our trials, but we did have Jesus. In many ways, we were forced to be available for the work of the Lord. God may have used your trial to provide you with a specific skill that He may want you to use someday. The art of being "available" is the art to move at a moment's notice, when God places a call upon you. And when that call comes, you hopefully will respond like Isaiah and proclaim to the Lord, "Here am I! Send me!"

Teachable

There is one person who instantly comes to mind when I think of teachable, any guess who? The apostle Peter. There is no other apostle that most demonstrates the idea of being teachable. Time after time Jesus rebukes him for being brash, quick to speak, and slow to listen. He appears to be a man who always knew the direction to go, the first to answer a question someone had; and yet, Peter was called from the seashore at Galilee to follow Christ to whatever end. He was the first out of the boat when Jesus called the disciple to get out of the boat to walk on water in Matthew 14. In Matthew 16, Jesus was talking about His anticipated suffering and crucifixion when Peter took Jesus aside and told Him in verse 22, "Far be it from you, Lord. This shall never happen to you." We may slightly disagree with the Lord from time to time, but to flat out rebuke Jesus is a whole other game. But this is Peter, and we are not surprised that Peter knows what needs to be done and how it all needs to be done. He's got it!

Time after time, after Peter sticks his foot in his mouth, or speaks out of turn. Jesus graciously reminds Peter of what He wants him to do, how He wants Peter to act, and of who He is and why He has come. These are gentle, gracious reminders to steer Peter in the right direction. In the Garden of Gethsemane, as Jesus is being arrested, Peter draws out his sword and strikes one of the Temple soldiers, cutting off his ear. Peter, however, was not aiming for his ear, but his head.

Just like Peter we are people who are passionate for the Lord, but can be a bit misguided from time to time if we are honest with ourselves. After Jesus rose from the grave, He and Peter have a one-on-one discussion on the shores of Galilee. In many ways, Peter was grateful to have this discussion. He had betrayed Jesus, but now Jesus was going to make all right. He was also going to set Peter on a path where he and the other disciples will change the world. Peter had finally learned. Amazingly, Proverbs 9:9 fits so perfectly with the end of the conversation Jesus and Peter have: "Give instruction to a wise man, and he will be still wiser; teach a righteous man, and he will increase in learning." Peter had much to learn as you and I do. The beautiful thing about Peter, and each of us, is that God is not done with us. We all have a long way to go.

As your story takes on a ministry declaring the work of God in your life, consider being F.A.T., *faithful* to the Lord's calling on your life and ministry, *available* for whatever the Lord has in store for you, and *teachable* and willing to learn at the Lord's feet. This should be each Christ-follower's passion all of their days, fair and stormy days alike.

Go forth F.A.T. and eager to glorify God with your life!

29

One Faith,
One Touched, One Healed

"She had heard the reports about Jesus and came up behind him in the crowd and touched his garment. For she said, 'If I touch even his garments, I will be made well.' And immediately the flow of blood dried up, and she felt in body that she was healed of her disease."

~ Mark 5:27-29

———◆———

Something was broken; something was wrong. For 12 years, she suffered a flow of blood. She paid doctors more and more to find a cure, but a cure was nowhere in sight, and neither was her healing. With continual bleeding, she was religiously and socially impure, pushed to society's margins. She had no more money, no friends to speak of, there was no hope left for her. But she had heard of Jesus. She had heard He made the blind see, the paralyzed walk, even the dead live. Her desperation drove her to the man Jesus. The crowds surrounding Jesus could not stop her. She quietly worked her way through the crowd. She had not been the focus of anyone's attention for 12 years, and she did not want to be a cause of disruption for Jesus or the crowd. She said to herself, "If I touch his garments, I will be made well."

In her humility, she approached Jesus, near enough to touch the hem of his garment. One moment she touched the hem, and a moment later, she felt like she had not felt in 12 years, healed, free, saved. It was not her intent to cause a raucous in the crowd; she just wanted to be quietly healed and go on with life as a new woman, healed, anew. But Jesus, when He heals, does not just heal, He saves!

The moment she touched his garment, He stopped, questioned the crowds, "Who touched my garments?" There are dozens of people around Him all jostling for a spot to hear Him speak, to ask Him a question, but this was a special someone who touched His garment. He knew who she was, and her affliction, but He needed to address her. The woman approached Him, confessing it was her, embarrassed that she had been called out because of her ailment. She fell before him and told Him everything. He was not mad, but looked down at her, proclaiming loudly to her that the entire crowd may hear, "Daughter, your faith has made you well; go in peace and be healed of your disease" (verse 34).

She believed that Christ could heal her, and more importantly, she believed He was the Son of God, her Savior. She knew that He healed her not just of her physical disease, but also her spiritual disease, sin. She came to Jesus because He was Messiah, He was the One who would save the world. He was the One she had heard of since being a child in the Jewish faith. If there was anyone in the world who could help her physically and spiritually, it was Him.

Her healing, like yours, was at the hands of Jesus Christ, at His will. Consider her life after this divine encounter. She went back to her hometown. She had left her town on the margins of society. Because of her illness, she was unclean, and society would not interact with her. She returned clean and with a magnificent story to tell. Most of the people Jesus heals take His healing and go. Two chapters later in Mark 7, Jesus heals a deaf man and says in verse 36, "And Jesus charged them to tell no one. But the more he charged them, the more zealously they proclaimed it." People could not stop speaking about what Jesus was doing.

What does this mean for us? You and I have been healed by Christ, most likely not miraculously, but nonetheless, Christ has purposed your storm to end. We are healed, the storm is over. What happens next?

The woman could have gone back to her life not saying anything to anyone about her healing, but she could not just go back to the life she had. Her life had forever changed that the people who knew her, even those who did not, heard of the majesty of Jesus Christ in her life.

So, what do we do now that our healing is over? For me, as a very imperfect person, I was amazed at what Jesus had done in my life. More than healing through the suffering of surgeries, radiation, and chemotherapy, I saw God at work in my life, my church, and many who were in my sphere of influence. I praise God for what He has done in the lives of many who walked this road with me, and many who have read *Anchored in the Storm*. I say that not for my own attention, but like this woman in this passage that has enthralled me for years, I could not be silent about what happened. I came out of my storm the same saved sinner I was before, but I knew God was present in every step of that journey with brain cancer. My prayer for you is that you find a way to exclaim the work of Jesus Christ in your life.

You have faith in Christ! Christ touched you! You were healed through Christ!

30

Given Today

"Brothers, I do not consider that I have made it my own. But one thing I do: forgetting what lies behind and straining forward to what lies ahead. I press on toward the goal for the prize of the upward call of God in Christ Jesus."

~ **Philippians 3:13-14**

———◆———

Think back with me for a moment back to a conversation, discussion, or argument you had with someone. Most likely, you can recall the setting, the words, maybe even the smells of these conversations. Can you remember any of the conversations, discussions, or arguments more than others? Do you dwell over words spoken? Do you chew and gnaw on the past, running through things again and again and again through your mind? I admit that I do. I sometimes cannot move on because the past hinders me. Not only does it hold my today, but it also holds my tomorrow and the ability to have a bright and unhindered future ahead.

As I thought about how as humans we tend to want to go back to the "better" life in the past, to relive "the glory days," to right some wrongs, to make different decisions, I thought of Lot's wife. It was odd when this story came to mind as we look to starting a fresh, new tomorrow as the sun starts to shine again. To make a long, biblical family story short, Abraham and his nephew, Lot, had parted ways. Lot took his family to live in the city of Sodom, one of the most sinful places in the world at the time, along with its sister city Gomorrah. God chose to destroy the two cities sending angels to warn Lot and his family to flee the city. The angels declare to Lot in Genesis 19:17, "Escape for your life. Do not look back or stop anywhere in the valley. Escape to the hills, lest you be swept away." The command was clear, "RUN FOR YOUR LIVES!" The angels warned Lot and his family to run, not to look back, not to consider what they were leaving behind, what of their possessions might survive, or to consider the memories made and kept there. The command was run, and they ran. "The sun had risen on the earth when Lot came to Zoar. Then the Lord rained on Sodom and Gomorrah sulfur and fire from the Lord out of heaven. And he overthrew those cities, and all the valley, and all the inhabitants of the cities, and what grew on the ground. But Lot's wife, behind him, looked back, and she became a pillar of salt" (Genesis 19:23-26).

We could speculate as to why Lot's wife looked back. Was she mourning her home and possessions? Was she thinking of the fond memories she and her family had? Was she considering the conversations both good and bad she had while living in Sodom? Was it the good times (or sin) the people of Sodom and Gomorrah were having and her memories amongst the people? Was it something in her past that she was holding onto, to peer over her shoulder one last time?

Lot, his wife, and his daughters were fleeing God's wrath, but Lot's wife was holding onto what God had declared His judgment on the city. Lot's wife was holding onto the past, and her consequence for disobeying the Lord was being turned into a pillar of salt.

It may be a loose connection, but it stood out to me as I considered the past of my own joys and trials throughout my own life. Sometimes I dwell on what the past was, ignoring the present and the possible future. It was not that the past presently holds me back, but I can remember a handful of times and circumstances where I dwelt and dwelt and dwelt on words someone said or did not say or words I said or did not say. I have looked back on the past wishing things might be different. Not only did those thoughts and rewinds in my mind really hurt time and time again, but they prevented me from having a wonderful present in time, the now, where I might have worked through these not just in the moment, but for the future. In praying through these situations with the Lord, I quietly laid them at His feet, leaving them there, and not holding onto them anymore.

But what does this have to do with Lot's wife? Lot's wife was so preoccupied with what lay behind her that she forgot to do what God had commanded, to move on towards a better future. You are not going to be turned to a pillar of salt like she was, but what holds your heart? What keeps your heart static and stalled in place? What is stopping you from moving on into the strong will and paths of the Lord Almighty? Our trials are a great weight on our souls, and they certainly are not easy paths to go down in any way. And whatever trial we are facing, physical, relational, emotional, financial, we can hold onto our past hurting our present and future.

The Lord has given great grace to you in not turning you into a pillar of salt when He tells you to move on and not be held by past trials and past sins. As the Lord is calling you out of the storm at this time, consider what is holding onto your heart. The goal of coming out of a storm is to consider what the Lord is teaching you, how He wants you to grow, what He wants you to do. You cannot do any of those things if the past is hampering your recovery. This time of healing after the storm is an excellent time to let go of the past, to cherish the memories, to silence those past conversations, to make amends when they can be made, and move into the glorious will of God with a clean slate as His forgiveness gives.

Time to move on, cherish the present, and hope for the future, all guided by the gracious hands of the Lord!

31

From ... Through ... To ... All Things

"Oh, the depths of the riches and wisdom and knowledge of God! How unsearchable are his judgments and how inscrutable his ways! 'For who has known the mind of the Lord, or who has been his counselor? Or who has given a gift to him that he might be repaid?' For from him and through him and to him are all things. To him be glory forever. Amen."

~ Romans 11:33-36

———— ◆ ————

Throughout Paul's many books, there is one thing he exudes throughout them all, his love and passion for the Lord. In Paul's life, there is no priority greater than the Lord; even when he was in prison in Rome awaiting his execution, the Lord was everything to Him. And Paul, here at the end of Romans 11, declares such a statement about God: "For from him and through him and to him are all things." It is a statement that stands all on its own. There is nothing to add to those beautiful words. God is everything ... boom ... drop the mic and move on! It's such a glorious statement. Let us talk about each of those keywords: from, through, to and see what else we glean from the Lord and His control of all things through the pen of Paul.

From

Paul writes to the Corinthians in his first letter to them in 1 Corinthians 8:6: "Yet for us there is one God, the Father, from whom are all things and for whom we exist, and one Lord, Jesus Christ, through whom are all things and through whom we exist." The statement is almost the same exact one as he wrote in Romans. Let us focus on the "from" statement. "From whom are all things." It is an incredible statement about God and His role in creation, all the way through time down in history, even down to our very souls, in "Him are all things." The statement is resounding, "all things." There is nothing that has not gone through His hands down into our world, down into our lives. The encouragement from Paul is incredible. God is aware of each moment of our lives, each thing we will say, each thing we will do, each valley, each mountain. All things are from His hands.

As I have been writing, I have been asking myself this question, if He gives only good things to His children, how is it that these difficult times come from Him? How is sin a part of our world when it is so much against Him? Why do people die? None of these situations are what I would call "good." Is it just me thinking this? I wish you were here to confirm or deny my thoughts. Thankfully, at the beginning of the passage in Romans Paul gives us a clue. He writes at the end of Romans 11 in verse 36, "To him be glory forever. Amen." Yes, God loves His children so very much and would do anything for them, and a part of Him loving His children is His glory. I do not believe we can fully understand God's entire character and nature, but I think that even more than His love for us is His glory. He does everything, so He gets the glory and credit. God is not the cause of sin, death, and suffering, but in His sovereignty He has allowed it. I cannot say why God has chosen this way, but I can say that God's ways are far above my simple and ignorant ways, and I have to trust.

So when we hear from Paul that "from whom are all things," we have to trust the Lord that yes, all things are from Him, but we remember it with a caveat that all things are for His glory, and with the easy and difficult paths of this life that we can hold onto the truth that God is in every part of it.

Through

Throughout the letters written by Paul, there is this theme of all things coming from God. In Colossians 1:15-17, Paul writes to the church of Colossae, "He is the image of the invisible God, the firstborn of all creation. For by him all things were created, in heaven and on earth, visible and invisible, whether thrones or dominions or rulers or authorities – all things were created through him and for him. And he is before all things, and in him all things hold together."

Think about God's hands for a moment. I imagine strong, large, rough hands, not hands that are smooth having never touched a plow, or a saw, or even dirt, but capable, hardworking hands. It's through these hands of God that all things have been created and allowed; everything that has ever been made, either Heaven or Earth, has passed through His hands. Consider not just hands that make things, but hands that direct the course of events, the course of minds, leaders, and followers alike. Every single thing you made God is aware of. His hands are directing all things for His glory!

To

Paul ends the book of Romans, one of the most profound books in the Bible, truly in all of the written word, with a praise to God, a doxology. He praises God in Romans 16:25-27: "Now to him who is able to strengthen you according to my gospel and the preaching of Jesus Christ, according to the revelation of the mystery that was kept secret for long ages but has now been disclosed and through the prophetic writings has been made known to all nations, according to the command of the eternal God, to bring about the obedience of faith—to the only wise God be glory forevermore through Jesus Christ! Amen."

If Paul's heartbeat were recorded in words, it would be this verse. Paul's heart beats to glorify God through all parts of His life. Every heartbeat, every breath, every part of Paul's life is for the Lord. It is an extraordinary position that Paul presents. The storms, the beatings, the imprisonments he faced, the thorn in his side, and the prayers, joys, and toils of his ministry were all for Jesus.

These thoughts on God's work in Paul's life should help us consider the words we might say about God's work in our lives. Paul laid his life at the feet of the Lord, declaring he would do anything, go anywhere, say anything the Lord desired, all to the glory of God. I am not sure if I am in that position or anywhere near adopting a life like Paul's, but the conviction of Paul and His love for the Lord are extraordinary and convicting for us as we consider our faith and path out of the storm.

From, Through, and To God are all things! Hallelujah!

32

Rise and Walk

"When Jesus perceived their thoughts, he answered them, 'Why do you question in your hearts? Which is easier, to say 'Your sins are forgiven you,' or to say, 'Rise and walk?' But that you may know that the Son of Man has authority on earth to forgive sins' – he said to the man who was paralyzed – "I say to you, rise, pick up your bed and go home." And immediately he rose up before them and picked up what he had been lying on and went home, glorifying God. And amazement seized them all, and they glorified God and were filled with awe, saying, 'We have seen extraordinary things today.'"

~ Luke 5:22b-26

The story of the paralyzed man has amazed me since being a kid in Sunday school. I can even picture the flannel graphs and imagine the wonder of it all.

Imagine yourself in a dirty, dusty town. People are flocking to a home, and you stop to see what's going on. As you join the flock, you see all kinds of people, rich and poor, religious and irreligious, weak and strong gathered around this one house. As you approach the house, you ask someone what's going on, and they mention the man Jesus is at the house teaching.

The crowds around the house say that Jesus has come to town and is teaching. People come to hear His words, to see His miracles, and in the case of the Jewish religious leaders, to question Jesus's claim of being the Son of God. You are eager to hear and see this man, Jesus, and the miracles everyone is talking about.

You notice a group of men carrying a bed in the crowd, much like a cot. The man lying on the bed is paralyzed and has been for many years. His friends had heard of Jesus' powers and were eager to help their friend walk again. The house was so full there was no way for the group and the paralyzed man to get into the house to see Jesus and have the paralyzed man healed. The group was desperate to get to Jesus, but no one would move out of their way, not a single one. In their desperation for their friend, they came up with an ingenious plan.

In those days, houses had stairs on the outside so people could cool off on the top of the flat roofs. The friends climb the stairs of the house and start tearing and hacking at the roof. If they couldn't enter through the front door, they were going to make another way. They make a hole big enough for their friend's cot and lower him down into the crowded room with ropes. I can just picture all the people inside the house looking quizzically at the ceiling, wondering what's going on. They had to shelter themselves as dirt and debris fall down on them and then they see the paralyzed man dropped through the ceiling into the room.

Jesus, a man of compassion, looks at the paralyzed man, then up to his friend peering over the hole in the roof. People wonder what the interrupted Jesus is going to say. He quietly opens His mouth and unexpectedly declares, "Man, your sins are forgiven you." People look quizzically around thinking, "Wait, this is Jesus, who does miracles and can heal this man instantly, yet the first thing He says is, 'Your sins are forgiven you.' Does Jesus not know that this man came to walk again?" The crowd does a double-take and the Jewish religious leaders, the scribes and the Pharisees, take this moment to challenge Jesus. These leaders have been trying to challenge Jesus all day long, and here is their moment. In some ways, they want to steal the thunder from the paralyzed man and Jesus. The group rises up and asks in their hearts, "Who is this who speaks blasphemies? Who can forgive sins but God alone?" (Luke 5:21). Knowing their thoughts, Jesus responds in verses 22-23, "Why do you question in your hearts? Which is easier to say, 'Your sins are forgiven you, or to say, 'Rise and walk'? But that you may know that the Son of Man has authority on earth to forgive sins."

It was an extraordinary statement regarding sins and healing. The people had come to see Jesus perform miracles and heal this paralyzed man. Jesus sets the group straight that He had not come to heal, but He came to seek and save the lost (Luke 19:19). Though the scribes and Pharisees will question Him, they cannot deny the fact that Jesus speaks with authority, always from a position beyond what the religious leaders understand. No one had ever questioned them in such a way.

Jesus declares He has authority to forgive sins and then turns to the man saying with such great compassion in His voice, "I say to you, rise, pick up your bed and go home." At this point, the conversation regarding authority was over. Jesus showed up, put the religious leaders in their place, forgave sins, and sent the paralyzed man home walking on his own. The man rose, and as he picked up his bed, he left for home, "glorifying God." The man's heart was rightly placed in giving immense credit and praise for the work of Christ in His life. The crowd, in stunned amazement, watches the man walk out to join his joyous friends. Luke says in Luke 5:26 as the man walked out, "And amazement seized them all, and they glorified God and were filled with awe, saying, 'We have seen extraordinary things today.'"

The end of the story leaves us in the exact moment you and I are presently in; the trial is over, so what is your initial response. For some, the trial is over in a moment, like the paralyzed man did; for others, it may be a slow progression, but there will be that moment when one realizes the trial is over. Let us take a look at how the man paralyzed for years responded and may his example help us as we leave our trial.

Look back at the passage and consider how the man responds to his healing. He grabs his bed and leaves for home, glorifying God. For years this man was unable to do anything for himself, now there were no limits to his new found abilities and incredible joys. Upon his heart was a new song, no longer a song of desperation, but a song of exultation for Jesus.

What joy is in your heart as you consider the end of your trial? Can you glorify God for what He has done in your life? What words are on your mind as you dwell on healing?

What if you are still suffering? Some trials in our lives take years to heal, and the reality of life in our sinful world is that God may not allow healing to happen this side of Heaven. How do you respond? Can you sit here and glorify God for what He has done in your life?

The second thing we learn from the man is that he returns home. Imagine for a moment his hometown, dusty and dirty like the town he was healed in. He walks into town, past stores, and stalls of people he knew. In stunned amazement, the townspeople have no words to articulate what they are seeing. This man is now walking before them with the biggest smile they have ever seen. I am sure that everyone in the town followed him to his home, eager to hear his story.

Like the paralyzed man, your trial has given you a story to tell. If you look back on your trial, prayerfully and carefully, the Lord was at work. Maybe He worked quietly and softly, or maybe He worked significantly and loudly (of course, God's hand in our lives is always significant). Whether your trial was big or small, there is a story to tell because God worked in your life. He chose to work in your life, both for you and for His glory.

Venture forth into a healed life with words of God's glory and your story for the world to hear and glorify God too!

33

Preparing from the Peak

*""I waited patiently for the Lord; he inclined to me and heard my cry
… As for me, I am poor and needy, but the Lord takes thought for me.
You are my help and my deliverer, do not delay, O my God!"*

~ Psalm 40:1, 17

David does something extraordinary in Psalm 40. I cannot reveal it right now, but read through Psalm 40 and see if you figure out what I am talking about.

David starts the passage coming out of a storm. He takes verses 1-10 to praise the Lord for how the His work in the difficult circumstances David faced. Like other biblical figures, David tends to be impatient, like us in the 21st century, where we are used to immediacy in everything. Not knowing exactly what was happening before verse one, we can surmise that there is some impatience from him in his situation, as there is in so many biblical figures, save Jesus. They exhibited impatience in their suffering, just as we are impatient over the tiniest things in our instant answer and instant gratification culture. By verse 11 he realizes, "As for you, O Lord, you will not restrain your mercy from me; your steadfast love and your faithfulness will ever preserve me!" David remembered that God is going to work, he takes a deep breath, prays, and waits. Only God and David know how long David waits, but as God has shown time after time in

His Word, He is a faithful God, and He is faithful in answering prayers. David does not describe his prayers or his feelings towards God.

Throughout the first ten verses, David provides us with his response of praise as David exits his storm. He praises the Lord for the new song on his heart, a song of the Lord's deliverance and answered prayers. The Lord delivered him from the "pit of destruction" (Psalm 40:2) just as the Lord has delivered you from your circumstances to bring you to a new day, a new perspective, all from your trial.

Have you ever been in a situation where you want the world to know about something that has happened in your life? That is where David is in these verses. David has seen God work in such a way that he wants the world to know. All David wants to talk about is God, and the work the Lord has done in his life. He says in Psalm 40:5b, "I will proclaim and tell of them, yet they are more than can be told." In David's one circumstance in Psalm 40, he declares there is more to say about God's work in his life than can be told in an entire lifetime. From delivering David to giving him a new song, to answering prayers, David is almost speechless. Words just cannot come out of his mouth fast enough in his praise for the Lord. He wants the world to know the God he serves, and the work God does for those who are His.

How have you reacted to your situation as you come out of a trial? What would you say to someone who wanted to know about your trial? What would you say to someone who wants to know how the Lord worked in your suffering? Would you be as ecstatic as David was? He ends this first half of the psalm in verse 10 with, "I have not hidden your deliverance within my heart; I have spoken of your faithfulness and your salvation; I have not concealed your steadfast love and your faithfulness from the great congregation."

David transitions in the psalm in an extraordinary way that surprised me, and here is that extraordinary moment I started this passage off with. He's on the mountaintop praising the Lord for His presence and influence in his life, but David shifts his prayer to prepare for the next trial. When I realized the shift, I was reminded of something my pastor says all the time, "You are either entering a trial or exiting a trial." David moves from praising his deliverance to praying for deliverance. One trial ended, and another began between verses 10 and 11. David, in His heart, knows that God tends to work best when life is hard. He knows that just because one trial is over this does not mean that another trial will not come. From my side, it would be like me saying, "Because I have had cancer, I won't have any other trials in my life." David lives in a reality that He has to praise the Lord for His faithful work in his life, but also needs to be realistic that someday, sometime, however many days are between the two verses, there will be another trial, possibly smaller, but possibly even bigger than the first.

Our hearts get settled when life returns to normal. Hopefully, we have changed and learned throughout our suffering, but however much we fight, life has a way of returning to us. We return to old habits, our prayers grow thin, our devotions are less regular, the fight for the intimacy with the Lord we had during our trials grows. There are new prayers that need to be prayed over our lives for the same strong relationship we had with the Lord.

David's prayer regarding his new suffering should give us pause to lift up the days ahead and the difficult roads we will face in the coming months and years. It was so astounding because I had never focused on praying for what was yet to be learned and how the Lord still needs to teach me. I had never focused on asking for the words I need to continue to proclaim His glory and gospel to a world in need of His salvation. As each of us coming out of a storm, seemingly at the peak of survival, David realized that we cannot live on the mountaintop. It is not where life happens. Enjoy those moments of triumph that the Lord has proven Himself faithful to you. He has answered so many prayers in your life of bringing you through your harrowing circumstances, but take those moments and lift up a prayer for the next trial, the next storm when you are off the mountaintop and down in that dark valley again. Pray the Lord's presence and continued work in your life, that you may be a blessed vessel for His glorious gospel. One day you will be on that mountaintop of triumph forever, in Heaven, but today we face life on this earth.

Pray for the days ahead; stormy days are forecasted for all who believe!

34

God Given Testimony

"And this is the testimony, that God gave us eternal life, and this life is in his Son. Whoever has the Son has life, whoever does not have the Son of God does not have life."

~ 1 John 5:11-12

Every person, almost eight billion of us presently on this earth, has a unique story to tell. No two stories are alike. The ups and downs, particularly the downs, have a way of shaping and molding our lives. If we are honest with ourselves, we all dislike change, particularly to ourselves and the lives we have built. Change is a part of making our lives what they are, making you … you.

So here you are, presently coming out of a storm that came unexpectedly. Take a moment and look over the time you spent in the trial. How did your life change? How did your story change? How did you change?

Maybe you are like me, looking back over a year of cancer, and realizing that life would never be the same again. There is not any way I could return to the life I had before I heard the word "cancer." If we look over our lives thinking of the many trials we have endured, we see that each had a lesson to learn. Each trial has a purpose in it, but when your life and future are on the line, the changes seem to be greater - at least they did for me. I pray that every trial you and I go through, our hearts will be less and less tied to this world.

While I was finishing up radiation, my church made a video of my testimony of the Lord's work in my life. I ended my story with, "I have lost everything ... but Christ." One of the interesting things about that statement is that I had not lost anything. Financially, fighting cancer was expensive, but I still had my home and my job. Many of the relationships I had before were strengthened, but sadly, some were lost. My health was weakened and would never be the same, but I was alive.

So, what had changed? My perspective!

What held my heart to this world was weakened, and I saw that everything in this life, aside from Christ, was worthless, literally everything. Would I be willing to put all aside for the sake of Christ? Would you be willing to put all aside for God's will? These are still questions that go through my mind as I live my daily life.

Over the next year, the Lord led me to take the many verses, notes, and quotes I had accumulated while I was undergoing surgeries and treatments to write out my thoughts as I recovered, resulting in *Anchored in the Storm*. This was part of my testimony, the Lord's work in my life. As you come back to a life out of the storm, you have a story to tell. You have a testimony the Lord has given you to proclaim to a world in need of Him. What Christ did in my cancer was to start a fire in my soul, a story I needed to tell, a book I never intended or thought to write. My life had been so affected by the hand of God that my new ministry was to pray and write for those going through their own storms, and now their recoveries.

Your life is in Christ, a child of the Lord, and His story of love, faithfulness, and salvation is now your story. How are you going to tell the world about what God has done in your life?

35

Word with You

""Have you not known? Have you not heard? The Lord is the ever-lasting God, the Creator of the ends of the earth. He does not faint or grow weary; his understanding is unsearchable."

~ Isaiah 40:28

Have you ever been in a conversation with a friend when your friend mentions something from your past that you do not remember? Your friend cannot believe you do not remember what they are talking about. It was an epic memory. After a few minutes of your friend teasing you and your concentration on your memory, it comes back, you remember and then you, and your friend laugh about it.

Isaiah, in chapter 40, is our friend calling us out. "Have you not known? Have you not heard?" Isaiah is saying, "Don't you remember? You know this! You were there, a part of this!" While he is primarily calling out the Jewish people, He is also calling us out today. "Have you not known? Have you not heard?"

As our storms subside, our memory becomes less crisp, foggier. We forget certain truths we have lived and experienced. I admit that at times I have forgotten I had cancer. There have been times when I have heard of someone either personally, or someone in the public square gets cancer. I feel bad when I hear of anyone getting cancer and pray for them and the road they have ahead. I pray as if I have never had cancer, and then I get this little nudge from my-self. I almost hear my soul saying, "Um, Adam, remember you had cancer!" In these rare moments, I have had to chuckle at myself just a bit. I'm not laughing at my cancer or the struggles of another, but just the fact that I had forgotten for a moment something so big in my life.

We all need reminders, and Isaiah is reminding the Jewish peo-ple about their great, almighty God with whom they have had in their past an incredible relationship. Like I had forgotten such a huge experience in my life; they had forgotten the most significant relationship they have ever had, with God Himself. God's chosen people had forgotten Him. Isaiah reminds them of God, which is incredibly tragic for a people whom God has placed His name upon.

We are in the exact same situation when we start forgetting God's work in our lives. In my forgetting the cancer, I almost for-got the great things God had done through the cancer. It is almost like God's work in my life and the cancer go hand in hand for the greatest experience I have ever had with God. Our memories of God's work in our lives are a great reminder for us to press on through the storms and calms of our lives because we can look back at how God has worked in the past. He provides a wonderful reminder of how He is going to work in the future.

And we know and have experienced the last part of Isaiah's verse, "He does not faint or grow weary; his understanding is un-searchable." This is the God we remember!

36

Completion

"And I am sure of this, that he who began a good work in you will bring it to completion at the day of Jesus Christ."

~ Philippians 1:6

———◆———

On the day you became a follower of Jesus Christ, God began a good and mighty work in your life. His work continues day in and day out, moment by moment, with each breath and heartbeat throughout your life. It is a work that is never done until we go to Heaven, and even then, I think we have an eternity ahead of us getting to know God.

It is hard to think of our suffering as a good work of God in our lives, but my prayer for you is that you will see your past trial, whether recent or in your distant past, as a good gift from the Lord of growing closer to and more like Him. Part of God's good work in our lives is the good work He does through suffering. It is almost like God's clarion call upon our lives to pursue His work in our lives, the lives of others and the life of His kingdom, and those who are to yet to be in the kingdom.

God's calling on the totality of your life is sanctification, to make you like Him, through the storm and the Son. Paul writes in 1 Thessalonians 5:23-24, "Now may the God of peace himself sanctify you completely, and may your whole spirit and soul and body be kept blameless at the coming of our Lord Jesus Christ. He who calls you is faithful: he will surely do it." God wants to sanctify you completely: spirit, soul, and body. What God starts; He will finish.

Over the years, after my cancer diagnosis, I continue to seek the Lord knowing that I am nowhere near completion. Paul reminds me that what God has started, He will finish. Unlike myself and so many others who start a project and years later it is still sitting there in our house, unfinished, and covered with dust, God will finish what He starts. God is a God of completion. There are no unfinished works in His kingdom and creation. The Lord's work may be imperceivably slow, stalled, or stopped, but God is continuously working when it seems otherwise. He is always working, even when we have given up on completion. And part of God working towards completion is that He works at full force until all is done, whole, complete, permanent, in God's words … perfect.

As a follower of Christ, a family member of Christ, sealed in the Holy Spirit, remember that God wants you to be like Him, perfect. And until that day comes when He calls you home to be with Him, He will tirelessly work toward that goal.

"And I am sure of this, that he who began a good work in you, will bring it to completion at the day of Jesus Christ."

37

Mountaintop Valley

*"I lift up my eyes to the mountains – where does my help come from?
My help comes from the Lord, the maker of heaven and earth."*

~ **Psalm 121:1-2 (NIV)**

———•◆•———

One night while I was drifting to sleep, I was dwelling on suffering in the valley. It seems natural for us to consider the valley a place of suffering. Psalm 23:4 says, "Even though I walk through the valley of the shadow of death, I will fear no evil, for you are with me; your rod and your staff, they comfort me." When we suffer, we often say we are going through a valley of cancer, a valley of financial burden, a valley of relational difficulties. The valleys of suffering are limitless in this world, and truly, the valleys of this earth are the lowest places we can get. Suffering takes our eyes off the plethora of distractions in our world and helps us to focus on our relationship with Christ. But are these valleys of suffering the only places of suffering?

As I drifted away sleepily, I suddenly awoke thinking of Moses on Mount Sinai with the Lord in Exodus 34. I considered whether the valley could truly be the mountaintop. For a moment, dwell on the writer's position of Psalm 121. He is clearly in the valley in need of help, but consider for a moment where the psalmist looks. He does not look around himself in the valley of suffering.

He does not look to others who are suffering with him, though we need people with us when we suffer. He says, "I lift my eyes to the hills, where does my help come from?" Help comes from where the Lord is. Healing comes from where the Lord is.

Exodus 34 is worth a thorough read. As you read, consider the time Moses and the Lord had together. The Lord called Moses to come up Mount Sinai alone. No one but Moses. No family, no servants, no guards, just Moses. With him he carried two blank stone tablets on which the Lord would inscribe the Ten Commandments. The Lord wanted to discuss the path ahead for the people of Israel, the Lord's chosen people. As Moses would attest and the Lord confirm, the people of Israel at this time were an idolatrous, grumbling, unsatisfied people who would remain so for centuries to come. Still nonetheless, the Lord chose them to be His people with whom He would declare His glory and salvation through all mankind in His Son, Jesus Christ.

Our sufferings are very much like Moses and the Lord on the top of Mount Sinai. Moses, for a time, is taken away from the life he knows as the leader of the Israelites. The Lord took this time with just He and Moses so the two of them could talk. The Lord had wanted him to better understand the will of God, and the purpose the Lord had for Him in bringing about salvation. This talk is transformative for Moses, who literally shows the effects of seeing God on his face, a glorious brightness, pouring off of him. Moses comes down from the mountain renewed to take on the task assigned to Him by the Lord, to reestablish the Israelites as the Lord's people and to take them on the journey to the Promised Land.

Your suffering has taken you from the daily routine, in some ways, and the Lord desires to take these valleys and refine us and make us more like Him. But here is where the mountaintop experience comes in. We would undoubtedly attest that we are in the valley of suffering, but our time with the Lord is the mountaintop experience.

God has called us out of our daily lives to focus on our relationship with Him, to depend and lean upon Him, and to understand our role and purpose in His kingdom. It is our unique experience with the Lord just as Moses had a unique experience with the Lord. Though our story and place is completely contrasted with Moses, the intimacy with the Lord is not. Our God is a very personal God. He wants to know His people, wants to be intimately involved in their lives, and wants His people to depend on Him as a child does their father. This is the beauty of the mountaintop valley.

As you exit your trial, you are coming up from the valley of suffering, but are also descending the mountaintop where you and God had a rich and refining time together. Moses comes down the mountain with his face glowing from meeting the Lord. As you come down, are you eager to share with others what God has done? Are you excited about encountering the Lord in such a personal and intimate experience? As Moses brought those tablets down to the people, are you bringing your testimony of the Lord's handiwork in your life to those in need, to those who need your experience with Christ to find salvation in Christ alone?

Come out of the fog and clouds and descend from the mountaintop eager to take on a new life, a new purpose, a new story all for the sake of Jesus Christ!

38

Worst News, Best News

"Believe in the Lord Jesus Christ and you will be saved."

~ Acts 16:31

W hat is the worst news you have ever received? Think back. How did you feel when you heard the news? What did you do moments after?

What if there was news you have never heard because someone was too afraid to tell you? What if in that bad news the person also held good news, but because they were too afraid, you never heard either news, the worst, and then the absolute best? How would you feel? So often in western society, even in the church, we are afraid of being honest and open, partly because of how a reaction may be received. We aren't willing to put ourselves on the line for the sake of someone else. Consider every Sunday morning at church, everyone looks so good and is doing so great!

Paul David Tripp writes in his Christmas devotion, *Come, Let Us Adore Him*, "The baby in the manger came to tell us the worst news ever, because until we accept the worst news ever, we'll never want the best news ever." As I have been asked throughout several of my doctor appointments over the years, "Do you want the bad news or good news first?" It makes me chuckle because either way, I'm going to get hit with both.

Here is the bad news, first for the world, and then for us: We have chosen throughout our life to live a life in opposition to why we were created. We have chosen to do both good and bad. Maybe we have thought we are good enough to go to Heaven, but the truth is that without Christ, we are not saved and will not be going to Heaven. For some, it may shock you that it is Christ and Christ alone, simple, pure, and true. Jesus Christ is the only way to Heaven.

The worst news continues. Many of us have thought that we believe in Christ, but we have deceived ourselves. We may go to church; we may even serve in the church. There is no life in our lives, there is no faith, we just go through the motions just checking boxes. I say this so that we all seriously consider our standing before the Lord and whether we are truly in Christ, going to Heaven, or if we will be separated from Christ literally forever, until the end of time ends, which will never happen.

We hate the word "hell," and the reality of hell is that the absolute worst part of the suffering we will face there is the eternal separation from the Lord. While alive on this earth, God has given us what we call common grace, His grace poured out on all mankind, the good, the bad, and the horribly evil. We often wonder why the good suffer and the evil prosper. God's common grace has made life better, though we are all under sin and condemned to hell. I think one of the hardest situations will be for those who knew Christ in knowledge, those who attended church for years, decades, maybe their entire life. However, at the end of their days, they have not accepted Jesus Christ as their Lord and Savior and have not surrendered the entirety of their lives to Christ.

So, there is the worst truth you could ever hear; you are going to hell ... without Christ. Take a few moments to truly, humbly, consider the reality of your salvation. So, what if you are not saved? Do you want to be saved? Paul tells the Philippian jailer in Acts 16:31, "Believe in the Lord Jesus Christ and you will be saved" and in Romans 10:9, "If you confess with your mouth that Jesus is

Lord and believe in your heart that God raised him from the dead, you will be saved." Here is a prayer you can say before the Lord, just the two of you:

Father,

Here I am, realizing that I have no standing before You without surrendering everything to You. Since birth, I have chosen to live life on my own without You. In my sin, I have acted against You, not wanting to know You. In my present sin, Lord, You have called me to salvation in You, and it is time for me to know You as my Lord and Savior. With all that I am, I believe that Jesus came to earth, 100% God, and 100% man. I believe that Jesus died on the cross, taking my sin, and dying for my disobedience in my place. I believe that Jesus rose from the dead three days later. You are my Lord and Savior and I long to live a life as Your creation reunited with You, my Creator! Teach me and lead me, I pray, Lord, into a life, where I can sin less and walk in Your will more.

In Your precious name, I pray! Amen!

Congratulations! You are, a follower of Christ, and a brother or sister to so many amazing people who are not perfect in any way, but they press on towards the higher calling of salvation, eagerly seeking God's glory. In the worst news of declaring to the Lord that you are a sinner, you have accepted the best news; Christ is your Savior. And no matter how great your sin is, God's grace is always greater. Your final place for eternity is no longer in hell, but the best news is that you will spend an eternity in heaven with God, living a life without sin, as God fully intended from the dawn of creation. Tripp was right; you and I needed to hear the worst news before we could hear the best news.

I admit that I am not as bold a witness as I need to be, and maybe, no matter how long you have been saved, you are finding the same thing about yourself. But we must be alert; we must not grow complacent in our walks, settling into a comfy and cozy relationship with the Lord. Our comfort and coziness in Christ is in Heaven; it is not here on earth. It is time for us to rise up and share Christ throughout our lives. I heard the saddest statement a while ago and cannot remember who said it, but it says a lot about the inhabitants of our world, "This is the only Heaven the unsaved will ever face, and in Christ, this is the only hell you will ever face." It certainly is not bad for those of us in Christ. But consider the first part about the only Heaven some will face is heartbreaking. This broken world, sinful and suffering in its own right will be the only goodness, if you could call it goodness, the unsaved with ever face. I cannot imagine that the saddest thing that our hell on this earth is the only Heaven many will ever see.

Let us venture out in our faith, renewed in our spirit, to eagerly take the gospel to our families, friends, and coworkers as Peter writes in 2 Peter 3:9, "The Lord is not slow to fulfill his promise as some count slowness but is patient toward you, not wishing that any should perish, that all should reach repentance."

39

God ... Over ... Me

"Then God said, 'Let us make man in our image, after our likeness....
So, God created man in his own image, in the image of God he created
him; male and female he created them."

~ **Genesis 1:26b-27**

———◆———

D o you like crowds? Throngs of people in the same place all headed in the same direction as you or blocking your way to where you are going. Have you ever taken a seat and just watched people for a moment or two? I find it amusing to sit there, at an airport, shopping mall, even Disneyland, to see how people interact with others. I consider their stories and where they may be off to, what they say to each other, and how they act.

In many ways, people are quite extraordinary creatures: good, bad, serious, silly, normal, and odd. Mankind stands out compared to the other creatures in this world. There are close to eight billion people on this earth, and while there can be striking similarities in some, there are billions and trillions more differences between us all. Above all, amid the almost eight billion of us, each of us at some point considered ourselves above the rest. It's astonishing how important we regard ourselves. At the top of the world and food chain, mankind sits with an astonishing misunderstanding of his place among creation.

When we look at it all, from a galaxy to an atom, can we honestly say that men and women are truly supreme over everything? Are we even supreme over our own lives? Does it not seem like there are so many things outside of our control? In our homes, our jobs, our lives, we think we can control everything, but even something as small as the common cold or a bad day at the office can bring us down. We control so very little, and in those moments of discomfort and suffering, we realize that we do not know it all and clearly do not have this life figured out. We are quick to forget our lack of control when we are back to our regular lives and "king of the mountain" again.

I can imagine God sitting up in Heaven, chuckling, laughing, and looking at us as an endearing father does his toddler. He knows that time after time, we continue to strive for our own greatness and preeminence over others. He knows that each of us, down to the depths of our sinful hearts, wants to be #1 in our lives, and as Christ-followers, we will continue this fight of who is in charge of our lives until the day we die. The reality of this inner struggle of control comes down to this: who are we going to let be over us? If we are honest with ourselves, we can look back and remember when we said, "I've got this" or "I know how to do it," only to realize that we do not have it, and we do not know how. We do not say it aloud, or even to ourselves, but we realize that we are not #1.

As we exit our storms, the great opportunity is that we get to put ourselves in the correct position. God ... over ... me. God first, you and me second. He is supreme, you and I are not. We were given a great gift in our suffering to realize, even in small trials, that we have almost no control over our lives (other than our free will, of course). Still the beautiful reality of our relationship with Christ is that He has it all under control. AMEN!

It is hard as the storm subsides, and we start our "new normal life." We get distracted by life in this world. Slowly over time we think we are in control again, we are the man, and once again, we have placed and declared ourselves "king of the mountain." The fight for survival during our storm is over, and the fight within our souls to ensure that God is in the correct position and priority in our lives is on. The fight is on to allow the Lord to have His rightful place over our lives. And when God is in His rightful place, all things work out for our good and His glory.

God ... over ... Me!

⚓ ⚓ ⚓

40

On the Line

"So Abraham called the name of that place, 'The Lord will provide;' as it is said to this day, 'On the mount of the Lord it shall be provided.'"

~ **Genesis 22:14**

———◆———

What is your most precious possession, the one thing you would have to take before leaving your burning house? Why is it precious to you? What would it take for you to give it up? Abraham was faced with a similar situation in Genesis 22.

One day God called on Abraham and Abraham, having encountered and talked with God over the years of his sojourn, said, "Here I am." It could have been an "I'm right here, Lord" or like Isaiah in Isaiah 6, an exuberant exclamation, "Here am I! Send me." Either way, God has a call on Abraham, and how Abraham acts will say everything about his faith in the Lord. God had chosen Abraham to be the vessel through which the world will be blessed. He had seen the Lord fulfill His promises, that of a son in his old age with his wife, Sarah. Abraham had no doubt seen God would work in ways that you and I can only read and dream about, but here Abraham is confronted. Abraham responding, "Here I am." to God's call will lead him on a journey he is never going to forget.

God told Abraham to take another journey. He says, "Take your son, your only son, Isaac, whom you love, and go to the land of Moriah, and offer him there as a burnt offering on one of the mountains of which I shall tell you" (Genesis 22:2). "What a curious statement?!?" Abraham left early the next morning with Isaac, two of his servants, and wood for the sacrifice. Abraham must have been mulling over this request as he prepared for the journey to Moriah. "Offer my son as a burnt offering? Did I hear God, correctly?" His mind must have been chewing over those words throughout the journey. What does this mean? God really does not mean 'offer him there as a burnt offering'?" But Abraham had seen God work mighty wonders over the years, and if God was asking him to sacrifice Isaac as an offering, there must be a purpose beyond his understanding.

The group arrived at Moriah, Abraham eyeing the place of sacrifice from afar. Still wondering how the Lord was going to work, he placed the wood for the burnt offering onto Isaac. Isaac would literally carry the wood of his own sacrifice and death on his back. The two of them climbed Moriah, in silence, Abraham dwelling on his son, the promised fulfillment of God, yet now God was calling Abraham to sacrifice his son. They reached the spot, and Isaac asked, "Behold, the fire and the food, but where is the lamb for a burnt offering?" (Genesis 22:7). Being a child, Isaac would not necessarily be able to understand God's call on his father, Abraham, and being a good father, Abraham would not have revealed the truth of the sacrifice. Abraham's breathing must have been heavy, not sure how to respond. Tears in his eyes he replied, "God will provide for himself the lamb for a burnt offering, my son."

In what had to be a moment of desperation, Abraham exudes incredible trust in the Lord. He had told Isaac the Lord would provide, and while Abraham was ready to offer Isaac, He also knew that God had plans beyond his own understanding. God had worked in Abraham's past, and God is going to work in Abraham's present.

They arrive at the spot. Abraham builds an altar to the Lord, lays the wood Isaac carried on the altar, and he binds Isaac. I can only imagine the torment in Abraham as he ties Isaac up. We have no idea as to how Isaac reacted to the situation. Scared, speechless, beside himself, we can only guess. Either way, Abraham puts Isaac on the altar, ready to sacrifice his promised son for the Lord. He lifts his knife high in the air ... and an angel of the Lord appears, declaring, "Abraham, Abraham!" Turning around, the angel says, "Do not lay your hand on the boy or do anything to him, for now I know that you fear God, seeing you have not withheld your son, your only son, from me" (Genesis 22:21). In great relief, Abraham took a few slow breaths and looked around, and there, caught in the thicket, was a ram. As the story closes, Abraham names the place of sacrifice, "'The Lord will provide,' as it is said to this day, 'On this mount of the Lord, it shall be provided'" (Genesis 22:14).

What seems like an odd request of the Lord was really a test for Abraham. Did Abraham love God more than his son? The question is the same for us, "Do I love _____ more than I love God?"

In our trials and storms of this life, where we can lose so much, is God's call upon our hearts, to evaluate our lives and consider what we love more than our love for Him. When the fire comes to your house, what are you taking? Or can you walk away knowing that God has it all? That you can walk away empty and penniless, and yet in Christ, be the richest person on the face of this earth. The question is, what is keeping you from your relationship with God? It could literally be anything. As you consider what the Lord was calling you to put on the line during your suffering, dwell on what still holds your heart, what you will hold onto over God.

God will respond however, God is going to respond, working mysteriously in many aspects of our lives to fulfill His will and purpose of His will. He may or may not respond to your sacrifice and willingness to lay down at His feet that which holds you. Still, He does respond to Abraham in Genesis 22:16-18, "By myself I have sworn, declares the Lord, because you have done this and have not withheld you son, your only son, I will surely bless you, and I will surely multiply your offspring as the stars of heaven and as the sand that is on the seashore. And your offspring shall possess the gate of his enemies, and in your offspring shall all the nations of the earth be blessed, because you have obeyed my voice."

At the end of it all, God held Abraham's heart and nothing more. May God hold your heart for this journey of life to do whatever the Lord desires!

41

Words of Life

"A gentle tongue is a tree of life, but perverseness in it breaks the spirit."

~ Proverbs 15:4

———◆———

All of us, to some extent or another, have been bullied or picked on at some point in life. Remember the kid that bullied you out on the playground or on the school bus. He or she would say something petty and mean, and you would reply, "Sticks and stones may break my bones, but words will never hurt me." You smugly yelled those words, turned around, and walked away proudly as if you were not hurt. But as you walked away, you knew those words did hurt, they did sting, and they did last, even years after. Maybe even now, those stinging words remain in your mind.

Even as adults, we may be maligned over someone's false claim, but sometimes even the truth hurts, and as we hear those words spoken, that old playground saying goes through our mind. You don't say it aloud, but you think it, and you wish those words were true. Those words sting just as much as when you were running around the grade school playground.

David writes of a similar experience in Psalm 57:4, "My soul is in the midst of lions; I lie down amid fiery beasts—the children of man, whose teeth are spears and arrows, whose tongues are sharp swords." David was fleeing Saul's persecution against him. Saul had spread lies and accusations, verbal spears, arrows, and swords against David and now was pursuing David's life. David's words fit so perfectly in describing the words of an enemy. They pierce, cut, and slice not physically as Saul wanted to do to David, but maybe even more tragically, our souls. These words themselves are a trial all on their own. They take away from life.

In verse 4, David laments his persecution, yet in a moment's time, turns to the truth of what he knows, He turns to the Lord declaring in Psalm 57:5, "Be exalted, O God, above the heavens! Let your glory be over all the earth!" David could write against Saul and his other enemies, calling them names, telling lies about them, but there is a higher ground, beyond our playground "sticks and stones." Just moments after being maligned, David changes his focus. He turns from the evil words said against him to praising God and how he feels about God. His words are beautiful, giving life and reviving the soul.

Our words carry such weight, and we so often throw them around, without any thought that words bring life and death. David chose the higher ground to speak words of life, praises to the Lord, that build us up thousands of years later. The words said against you and to you may still ring true in your ear to this day and may remain there for years to come. But what words of the Lord will replace those bully's words in your soul? We may allow those memories to plague us, even the memories of suffering, but like David, we need to take those memories, those words, to the Lord and go to His Word for words of truth and life. It does not matter what someone says, especially if they are not true. What matters most is what the Lord would say about us.

In the calm, out of the storm, we can choose to accept words said against us, or we can evaluate any truth and leave them at the foot of the cross, ready to praise the Lord in life, declaring the beautiful truth of the Lord's work in our lives.

42

No Going Back

""Brothers, I do not consider that I have made it my own. But one thing I do: forgetting what lies behind and straining forward to what lies ahead. I press on toward the goal for the prize of the upward call of God in Jesus Christ."

~ **Philippians 3:13-14**

———◆———

One of the topics I have written throughout this book is that there is no going back to the life we had before the storm. Life has changed so much that I almost do not recognize life anymore, but not in a bad way, as if one part of life were better than the next. Each part of life has its ups and downs, its unique challenges along with its glorious triumphs. I admit there are some parts of life that time will not mend, things I had dreamed of years ago that I thought may happen in the future, but the reality is they may not. These times of calm allow us a perspective of briefly looking back, saying goodbye to what was, and embracing what is to come, whether good or bad.

J.R.R. Tolkien so wisely writes these thoughts through Frodo, the main protagonist, in his triumphant trilogy *Lord of the Rings: The Return of the King*, "How do you go on, when in your heart you begin to understand … there is no going back? There are some things that time cannot mend. Some hurts that go too deep." Frodo left an idyllic home and life, a life of comfort without any challenges or changes until he was confronted with an unsurmountable task to literally save the world. By the end of *Return of the Kings*, the last book in the trilogy, Frodo returned home, stories he will regale for years and wounds that physically will not heal, but there are also those emotional wounds; the journey he was on was beyond his strength. He realizes he will carry these wounds throughout the rest of his days, as you might carry your wounds. We don't carry them in the sense that we need to bring them out in each conversation or that we hold onto them, but in a sense that those wounds and scars are there and have a story to tell, as Frodo told his through Tolkien.

Life is not lost though, and life in no way is finished until that final call of the Lord. We have a life ahead, and Paul addresses this life after the storm in Philippians 3:13-14, "Brothers, I do not consider that I have made it my own. But one thing I do: forgetting what lies behind and straining forward to what lies ahead. I press on toward the goal for the prize of the upward call of God in Jesus Christ."

Our storm took a mighty toll on us; life will never be the same, and for many significant trials, it can never be the same again. But here we are on the other side facing a new life, a life we never expected, but life, nonetheless. What do we do with this new life? Paul couldn't have said it better. He knows Jesus lies ahead. Paul knows he can't go back to what was, no matter how good those past days were. He knows it is better ahead. The goal and prize of this life is Jesus Christ. In our new "normal" life that we have been graced with, we are to press on towards a better life, no matter the circumstances, to the prize of knowing Christ. In that ultimate day we will stand before Him, in all His glory.

There is no going back, just pressing forward. Press on to the heavenly calling of Christ towards the life best lived in Him.

43

Who God Is ... Over Who I Am

"Then Job answered the Lord and said, 'Behold, I am of small account; what shall I answer you? I lay my hand on my mouth. I have spoken once, and I will not answer; twice, but I will proceed no further."

~ Job 40:3-5

We humans have such a way about us, puffing our chests out as if our presence blesses the world. I have a little chuckle when I see someone walk into a room as if the world could not go on without them. Our pride in our own existence was our downfall in the Garden. Remember Adam and Eve; they fell (and thus we fell) because we wanted to be equal with God. We thought ourselves equal and on par with God, of the same standing as Him. We misconstrued the glory of God's creation, desiring that we could be the creator and tell God and the world what to do. We so quickly and easily forget that God is Creator, and every human is creation. There are roles in our relationship; one is superior, the other is inferior. Being inferior to God is not a bad place to be. The Lord is our heavenly Father, a Father who cares deeply for each of His children, each His precious creation. He wants only the best things for us. But as you and I can attest throughout our lives, we are eager to assert our position over the Lord all the time, and we consistently realize as the Lord regularly reminds us that He is God, and we are not. And that's a good thing! God keeps coming back and reminding us who He is over who we are, one of us is greater, and the other is lesser, so much lesser.

For most of the book of Job, our consummate book on suffering, Job and his friends spend their time discussing Job's place and God's place. They spend most of the time misinterpreting God, His creation, and the role of suffering in our lives. They may be trying hard to discuss man's role in God's world, but they can never get to the depth of the role and relationship God has intended for Himself and the people of His creation.

God was silent throughout the majority of the book of Job, the author choosing to focus on Job and his friends as they interpreted Job's responsibility for his calamities. Unheard from since chapter 2, the Lord declares His presence in chapter 38. He wants to set Job straight. He calls Job out in verse 3 of that chapter, "Dress for action like a man," essentially "put your big boy pants on!" Over the next chapters, God declares who He is over who Job is and subsequently who you and I are. It's an intriguing monologue because God asks question after question of Job, "Where were you when I laid the foundation of the earth? (38:4), many times goading Job to respond as in that same verse, "Tell me, if you have understanding." Later in the chapter, He asks Job, "Can you bind the chains of the Pleiades or loose the cords of Orion? ... Do you know the ordinance of the heavens? ... Can you send forth lightnings that they may go and say to you 'Here we are?'" Or consider this biting question in Job 38:36-37a, "Who has put wisdom in the inward parts or given understanding to the mind? Who can number the clouds by wisdom?" God is asking questions of Job that he could never answer. I imagine Job just sitting there stunned. What could he say in response?

It is a shocking monologue as God, throughout chapters 38-41 questions, Job, prodding him on to respond. Then we get to chapter 42, where God takes a break, leans back, and allows Job to respond. It is a humble response. "Then Job answered the Lord and said, 'I know that you can do all things, and that no purpose of yours can be thwarted. Who is this that hides counsel without knowledge? Therefore I have uttered what I did not understand, things too wonderful for me, which I did not know.' 'Hear, and I will speak;

I will question you, and you make it known to me.' I had heard of you by the hearing of the ear, but now my eye sees you; therefore I despise myself, and repent in dust and ashes" (Job 42:1-6).

God comes on the scene, strongly, and proudly defending who He is to put Job and his friends in their place. They had misrepresented God's nature and character, and God was quietly waiting for the perfect time to enter the scene and set things right with the men. We need these reminders of who we are and who God is. When we understand the relationship and role of God and we pray, we are put in the right position with God. We each have our roles to play, and as humans, we cannot play God; when we do, it is an utter failure. God corrects our thoughts on Him for our sake, that we may understand our place in the universe. There is harmony in life when we understand that God is over us.

Job 42:5 has become my verse coming out of my storm with cancer. I knew God before the cancer. I would say He and I were quite close. Like Job, I could now say, "I had heard of God," and I pray that you will say, "but now my eye sees you!"

44

A Home Unknown

"But according to his promise we are waiting for new heavens and a new earth in which righteousness dwells."

~ 2 Peter 3:13

D o you ever look at this world and just see and sense that something is not right? It is as if you know you are made for something else, to be someone else, for somewhere else. Even as an unbeliever, you know something is just not right when you look around, that at no point in human history has it ever been a perfect place. Even our lives and the struggles and sufferings that are common to all of us are just not right.

Throughout 2015, as I healed from my cancer treatment, I had the great sorrow of saying goodbye to many of the doctors and medical team that had been so crucial to my survival who were no longer a regular part of my life. It was a good thing to get back to real life, to return to life not as it was, but as I grew accustomed to saying, a "new normal." I was given a prognosis of five years before I was finally and officially diagnosed with anaplastic ependymoma grade III in 2015, with the prognosis changed to "We have no idea." Ependymoma is a tricky cancer because we know so very little about it. Each small headache, each day of feeling a little off, before each MRI, I often thought the cancer had returned, and then each medical report came back, and all was fine. And here as I write in the Fall of 2019, five years have passed by, seemingly free from the cancer that plagued me, but that five-year prognosis sticks quite loudly in the back of my mind. What plagues me most is not the return of the cancer, which may still reappear, it is the thought that something is not right in this world, as if I am meant for a completely different world, a completely different life.

You see, with each headache, each day of feeling a little off, each MRI, I thought the cancer had returned. My thought was not on the cancer, it was on the world I belong to. As a Christ-follower, you belong to the world completely under the control of Jesus Christ as He created it, not as our sin distorts it. This heartache of being in a world broken by sin makes daily living so very hard for the Christ-follower. It is not that I do not like my life in this world, trust me I do, but something is off; it always has been. It's this longing for what is to come that makes living difficult. Adapted and modernized from *Mere Christianity*, author C.S. Lewis said it perfectly, "If I find in myself desires which nothing in this world can satisfy, the only logical explanation is that I was made for another world." We are on this earth, but this earth, as it is in its present state, is not home, in any way. The world God created in Genesis 1 is not the world we know; it was a different world, a perfect world. The only world we know is one utterly corrupted and depraved by sin, for the moment under the control of Satan. You and I see glimpses of the world under God's hand when we read His Word and see His character. We do not know the specifics of a world completely under the Lord's hand, but we know He is in charge, and all things work together for good in the kingdom of Christ (Romans 8:28).

So, as I pass five years cancer-free, I look at it with mixed feelings. It is wonderful not to fight that terrible disease anymore, but it also means there is no clear picture of the path the Lord has me on as He leads me through life towards His glorious world, a world as it should be. The Lord and I have discussed this deep longing in my heart for Him, for a world under His permanent and gracious hand, for a perfect life under the yoke of Jesus. Hours and hours over the years, we have talked. God keeps telling me that while I long for heaven 24/7, He has not yet taken me home. We can waste life thinking about Heaven all the time. I am not saying the thought of heaven is bad, but the Lord keeps us on this earth for a reason and a purpose, a task for us to do now with the goal of Heaven in sight. On my bathroom mirror and computer at work is a reminder that keeps me moving on, "There is much to be done. Let's not lose sight." The Lord has much for us to do for His kingdom during our lives.

It is hard not to get distracted. This world, this home is all we know. And I admit that I try and try to make this world home, but no matter what I do, I know it's not home. I know it is not permanent, but here we are, this sin-soaked world is all we know, and we yearn and pine for the perfection that is Jesus.

While I long for a life outside this world, here I am, and here you are, living in this world. Our lives are not here to waste away as Isaiah writes of many sinners in his world as well as ours in Isaiah 22:13b, "Let us eat and drink, for tomorrow we die." The phrase seems to be the mantra of our present world. People live to get what they can from this world, from this life because without Christ, there is no tomorrow of joy, just an eternity of sorrow and suffering.

But, Christ-follower, hold fast, for if tomorrow you and I die, we will have life forever with the One who placed and sealed His Spirit in you, the One who just before the dawn of creation thought of you, the One who saw your face while He hung on the cross. He will come and take you to be with Him forever, in His presence, enjoying life under His grace and great pleasures.

The last words of John 14:3 (NIV) ring so true for the Christ-follower, "that you also may be where I am." At last, in the Father's home … forever. And let us make our lives in Christ significant in this world, but let us never make it home.

45

Your Thoughts, My Thoughts

"For my thoughts are not your thoughts, neither are your ways my ways, declares the LORD. For as the heavens are higher than the earth, so are my ways higher than your ways and my thoughts higher than your thoughts."

~ Isaiah 55:8-9

Have you ever questioned the "why?" of your suffering? It is not the "why me?" question, but the "why?" information-type question. It is a subtle shift from the "why me?" to understand the reasons behind the suffering. It is a question of purpose, intent, and meaning. More often than not, we are looking at the deserving or not deserving of suffering with the "why?" but there is a part that wants to understand our suffering and how something like this could happen. For the Christian, we might consider, "God, why are you doing this?" We know there is purpose in the biggest and smallest of circumstances, so what is it I can learn and know and become in this time of suffering? This type of "why?" question may be one you are just considering about your suffering or currently in your calm and recovery. What is the purpose behind this?

I look back on the past five years since hearing the word "cancer," and I can see clearly, not entirely, but more clearly, why I had cancer. You reading this book is one of the purposes of my cancer.

You play a part in my story as I play a part in your story. Do I understand the entirety of my suffering? Absolutely not!

Isaiah tells us the truth in the verse above of our "whys?" and of trying to understand our lives under God. And the truth is, we will never fully know the "whys?" God does things as God does things, the way He wants, in the time He wants, for the purposes He wants. In some ways, it doesn't seem fair because we do want to understand beyond our situation, but in other ways it tells us such a mighty thing about our God and our place before Him.

David writes about God's place and our place in Psalm 103:11-12: "For as high as the heavens are above the earth, so great is his steadfast love toward those who fear him; as far as the east is from the west, so far does he remove our transgressions from us." God gives us just enough information to understand Him, but we could never, at least this side of Heaven, fully know God down to the depths of His core. He has revealed Himself as much as He has because He wants us to know Him, but He is so wondrous we could not fully know Him. Remember, we are in a secondary position with God, and He is in the primary position. The way God works is not the way we work, and our understanding must be understanding God and our role under God.

Rest in the truth that God in His sovereignty knows the answer to "why?"

46

New, Not Old

"Therefore, if anyone is in Christ, he is a new creation. The old has passed away; behold the new has come."

~ 2 Corinthians 5:17

———————◆———————

It's a *Wonderful Life* is one of my favorite movies, and I admit to tearing up almost every time I see it, which is several times throughout the Christmas season. In one poignant discussion, the main character George Bailey, and his father are discussing life over dinner. Trying to help George understand why life was not going the way he wanted, watching life pass as other's are more successful, more popular, more influential, his father says to him in the last conversation the two would have, "Maybe you were born older, George." And just a moment later he says again, "I say you were born older."

While George's father is talking about George's wisdom and abilities compared with his brother. There is a truth in that statement, that we are all born old. We entered this world with an innate ability, equal to every single person ever born; we know how to sin. Sin, as old as Adam and Eve, has been a part of this world since the moment they disobeyed God. Sin is nothing new in this world or to mankind; it is an old, old companion of man. There surely are differences between George Bailey in a movie talking about life and us talking about old sin. You and George Baily, at a certain moment, are going to realize the newness of this life (and I admit that a film is hardly the perfect example, but bear with me until the end). At the end of the film, George is given a spectacular gift, a new perspective on his life. He has seen a world without himself in it, how the choices and decisions he made impacted the lives of so many around him. The movie ends, and we never find out how the new perspective George receives has changed his life, his family, and the small town of Bedford Falls.

The Apostle Paul gives us a stronger argument. In Galatians 5:17 he says, "Therefore, if anyone is in Christ, he is a new creation. The old has passed away; behold the new has come." As Christians, we are in a fight; our old sinful self is always trying to regain its power in our lives, to maintain its old power and control. Sin, seemingly as old as time in our world, is no more in Christ. As we prayed our prayer of salvation, surrendering all to Christ, trusting Him as our Lord and Savior, our sin of old was laid at His feet, and truly our old self was laid there as well. We were given a new life, a new perspective, and life that would never be the same again, no matter how much sin tries to sneak back in. As much as the old man or woman you and I were, we can trust from Psalm 103:11-12 that "for as high as the heavens are above the earth, so great is his steadfast love toward those who fear him; as far as the east is from the west, so far does he remove our transgressions from us." Before Christ, the old is gone, and the new has come. You are a brand new creation, born of the Spirit. In this new life, you have a new understanding of who you were, and now in Christ, who you are. The new will be as far from the old as the east is from the west.

As George Bailey got a new perspective on life, our storms have given us a new perspective in Christ.

47

Dawn and Dusk

"And we know that the Son of God has come and has given us understanding, so that we may know him who is true; and we are in him who is true, in his Son Jesus Christ. He is the true God and eternal life."

~ 1 John 5:20

A nyone that has known me for a long time, and knows a bit about my music tastes, knows that I love movie soundtracks. I do not watch too many new movies anymore, but I will often hear a song, and it just catches me. One of the songs that captured my heart while watching a movie was *On the Nature of Daylight*, is a sober song, but captivating song. It is an instrumental song that makes me see the sun rising and the sun setting. One evening while I was reading and listening to the song, something dawned on me. The song made me think of life; it was quite extraordinary.

Two days in our lives draw the greatest attention; the day we are born and the day we die. Everyone gathers at a birth to celebrate new life and at death to commemorate a life. Like the sunrise and sunset, we give more attention and memory to these days than most days of our lives.

Imagine: you wake up before dawn, head out to a peak with your coffee or tea, and sit there contemplating the sunrise. It is extraordinary to observe the colors that dance across the sky as the sun rises. Once the sun is up you go about your day, not noticing the sun's position, going about your business as if nothing extraordinary were happening. Later you head home and return to the same peak, but this time you have turned around, watching the sunset. No words are uttered as you consider the beauty before you, colors, and designs that not even the best artist in all of human history can replicate.

These moments of dawn and dusk may stay in your memory for years to come. The tragedy is that the day and the life lived during the day, while the sun coursed across the skies, will not stay in your memory. You may wake up the next morning remembering the sunrise and the sunset, but there is no recollection of the minutes and hours spent going about our business.

Our lives are very much like the sunrise and the sunset. We think our most important days are those when we are born and when we die, as if all those things we did in-between were of no consequence or significance. Yet our lives belong to the Lord and all those days spent without the extravagance or beauty of the sunrise and the sunset are those that may be the most important. Those are the day we lived, made decisions, shared the gospel, those days in-between our birth and death are of the utmost importance. My pastor shared the following quote in a sermon, and while attributed to Mark Twain, there is some dispute if he actually said: "The two most important days in your life are the day you are born and the day you find out why." In Christ, our "why" is Him. We were put on this earth and saved from our sin for His glory.

As we contemplate our role in this world as Christ-followers, we have to consider the days we have before our passing. Our passing into eternal life in the presence of God is going to leave us in awe, but for our short time on this earth, we need to consider our days between the sunrise and the sunset. Those two days are significant, to say the least, but each day is given to us by the hand of the Lord and is meant to be lived purposefully, for Him.

Consider your days between dawn and dusk. As dusk sets, what do you want painted across the sky of the minds, what impact will you leave in the hearts, and how will a life well lived impact those in and out of the kingdom that think back on the dawn, dusk, and all the days in-between of our lives.

48

A Life Empty ... A Life Full

"Nevertheless, I tell you the truth: it is to your advantage that I go away, for if I do not go away, the Helper will not come to you. But if I go, I will send him to you."

~ John 16:7

———— ◆ ————

For three years, the apostles followed Jesus, lived with Jesus, prayed with Jesus, learned from Jesus, and most likely laughed with Jesus. The entire time Jesus was with his disciples, He knew His time was temporary. He knew the outcome of His time on earth. He came to minister to the people of Israel, die for the sins of all mankind, rise from the dead, and leave earth to go home. God the Father had a bold plan, but as it is, we often struggle with His plans, especially when it does not fit our plan.

For the disciples, it was a double whammy. They had heard of and seen Christ arrested, tortured, and his death on the cross. He was gone; He died. They relished the day He rose from the grave and appeared, the meals they would all have together, the conversations. The disciples knew Jesus' presence was not permanent. He was leaving once again, for good. This was a huge loss for them and many struggled with what to do. They didn't know how to function without Jesus present with them regularly. Their closeness of three years left an empty space in their lives and souls. It is hard for them to fathom a life without Christ.

In our storms, we have lost so much, and some of us have lost those we love. To think that you will not see that person again, not hear their voice, feel their presence, talk with them is seemingly impossible to make sense of. But it is a reality we must face in all of our relationships at some point.

As the disciples contemplate life without Jesus, they recall a conversation with Him where He talked about sending someone to help in this time of loss. He says in John 16:7, "Nevertheless, I tell you the truth: it is to your advantage that I go away, for if I do not go away, the Helper will not come to you. But if I go, I will send him to you" (John 16:17). Jesus was preparing to leave in His ascension to heaven. The disciples remembered that while on earth, Jesus could only be in one place at one time; He was restricted by His physical nature, like you. He could not always be with each disciple as they spread the good news around the world.

But God, in His magnificent wisdom and plan, desired to fill that void of a relationship with His people. The Helper, the Holy Spirit, the third member of the Godhead, is always there, always present in the believer's life. No doubt it's great being in the presence of Christ, but the Spirit is God, God with you, actively working in your life, all parts.

What does all that mean for us grieving a loss of a relationship?

It may be hard to fully grasp, but the presence of the Spirit is better than that of a loved one. But what if the Spirit is more present than that loved one? What if the Holy Spirit is more present in your life than any relationship you have ever had or will ever have? Is this possible? For the Christ-follower, the answer is absolutely and resoundingly "Yes!" Our relationship with the Spirit is not like that of a relationship with a human. It is a human/God relationship, not a human/human relationship. How we interact with the Spirit is not how we interact with other people. So, how does one interact with the Spirit, your constant companion? Prayer! The Spirit is present with you always. In Romans 8:26-27, Paul tells us of the strengths of the Spirit. He says, "Likewise the Spirit helps us in our weakness. For we do not know what to pray for as we ought, but the Spirit himself intercedes for us with groanings too deep for words. And he who searches hearts knows what is the mind of the Spirit because the Spirit intercedes for the saints according to the will of God." When we do not always know what to pray or are praying outside God's will, the Spirit gives us incredible help by re-praying for us before the throne of God.

The Spirit is here, inside every believer. Embrace the work of God in your life through the work of the Holy Spirit! And lift to Him those prayers of your soul!

49

The Light Shines Again

"Arise, shine, for your light has come, and the glory of the Lord has risen upon you."

~ Isaiah 60:1

Our sufferings, our trials, our storms can seem so dark that we wonder about the end. We wonder when the light will shine again. The kingdom of Israel was in the same spot during Isaiah's day; the kingdom was in a perpetual decline, the Assyrian empire, among many empires throughout Israel's history, was a continual threat to Israel's existence. The Jewish people were a people split by tribes, not just in political decline, but spiritual decline. For Isaiah and other Jews who remained with the Lord, life was difficult. They believed God, but it was hard. Life was dark; life was a storm. The darkness of Israel's decline was disheartening.

Isaiah, as a prophet of Israel, was rarely popular, and his words to the Jewish people were not always well-received, if ever received. Above all, Isaiah wanted to do God's will. He wanted to bring the people back into relationship and obedience to the Lord, but the people were obstinate. He pressed on as a prophet, walking in the darkness of Israel's decline. But all hope was not lost and the darkness in Israel would not persist forever, just as our trial is not to last. The sun, through the Son, will shine again.

Even though Isaiah's days were dark, God's words were not always dark. He showed that it would shine for Israel once again, but also for Isaiah, for Gentiles, and for you and me. All of Isaiah 60 is about the light shining again, maybe not in this life, but certainly in Heaven. Read through Isaiah 60 and see that the hope of calm and peace would come in the future. Here are a few of the highlights of the light returning to Israel, to the Jews, and us:

- verse 2b: "But the Lord will arise upon you, and his glory will be seen upon you."

- verse 5: "Then you shall see and be radiant; your heart shall thrill and exult."

- verse 9: "For the coastlands shall hope for me, the ships of Tarshish first, to bring your children from afar, their silver and gold with them, for the name of the LORD your God, and for the Holy One of Israel, because he has made you beautiful."

- verse 19: "The sun shall be no more your light by day, nor for brightness shall the moon give you light; but the Lord will be your everlasting light and your God will be your glory."

- Verse 20: "Your sun shall no more go down, nor your moon withdraw itself; for the Lord will be your everlasting light, and your days of mourning shall be ended."

- Verse 21: "Your people shall all be righteous … the work of my hands, that I might be glorified."

And to end the chapter of light and restoration in verse 22 he declares, "The least one shall become a clan, and the smallest one a mighty nation; I am the Lord; in its time I will hasten it." In the presence of Jesus Christ, in Heaven, we will see the eternal light of God forever. Darkness will shine no more, and what we have lost will be found in Christ alone.

The reality of our lives in this world, even if we were not suffering, is that as long as sin remains in our world, our entire lives on this earth are under a shade of darkness. Until we see Christ's return or we go to Heaven we will not fully see the glory of God. Our brightest day on this earth will never be as bright as our darkest days in Heaven.*

*And the beautiful thing is that there are no dark days in heaven.

50

First Love

"I know your works, your toil and your patient endurance, and how you cannot bear with those who are evil, but have tested those who call themselves apostles and are not, and found them to be false. I know you are enduring patiently and bearing up for my name's sake, and you have not grown weary."

~ Revelation 2:2-3

---◆---

The apostle John was the only disciple of Jesus not to be executed, dying at an old age that we would envy even today. He played a special role in the church as the beloved disciple. In his decades since Christ ascended to Heaven, he had seen it all, the church expanded across the Mediterranean to Europe, south and west to Africa, and east towards Asia. He had seen and read the great authors of the New Testament, Paul, Peter, and of course, contributing the gospel and books that bear his name, John. He had also seen persecution rise towards the church; hundreds and thousands of Christians across the Roman Empire were being executed in horrific ways for the sake of Christ. John was exiled to the island of Patmos when the Lord brought him the words of Revelation.

Chapter 2 of Revelation starts with an analysis of the seven churches in the Mediterranean. The first was Ephesus. As an apostle, John had experience with each of these churches and holds them dear in his heart. The first church John wrote about, Ephesus, seems to receive one of the strongest commendations of any church in the New Testament. The church at Ephesus has toiled and worked hard. They endured persecution patiently, did not tolerate evil, tested those who say they are Christian leaders; they handled persecution well. These are amazing things to be said of any church.

But …

Then the Lord calls out the church at Ephesus. He commended them for all these good things, yet He says, "I have this against you" (Revelation 2:4). Imagine the Lord saying that to you. This church seemed to be on fire for God; everything seemed to be going well. The church, however, was not entirely committed.

What is it God had against them? These are some of the most stinging words in the Bible. God says, "You have abandoned the love you had at first" (Revelation 2:4). They had left their first love, the Lord. Focusing on all they were and had accomplished, they forgot Christ. The sad thing is that He literally meant nothing to them. They were interested in things other than the Savior.

But as always with God, the story does not end with His condemnation. Yes, they hurt Him desperately, but the Lord is not done with the church of Ephesus.

The Lord is gracious, committed, and forgiving to them. He is just as He calls them out. He calls them back to confess and repent and to know the work they did at first with their first love, Jesus Christ.

The passage in Revelation 2 starts beautifully, then takes a very dark and deep turn and then takes another twist to one of the most amazing gifts that are for those who are faithful and steadfast in their faith. The Lord says in Romans 2:7b, "To the one who conquers I will grant to eat of the tree of life, which is in the paradise of God." All is not over for the people of the church of Ephesus.

I can only imagine the taste of fruit from the tree of life. What a meal! And not just eating of the tree of life but present in the paradise of God. No mental image exists of this absolutely incredible meal with the Lord, but you as a Christ-follower will one day see and eat in the paradise of the Lord. Just imagine!

What does this mean for us as we come out of our suffering? Think about all the wonderful things people might say about you. They may talk of your strength, your witness, your courage (as they did about me when I was in my storm). But ... But... But... Like the church of Ephesus, God is calling each of us out, to examine ourselves, to confess, to repent, and to place Christ in the prime position of our lives.

We have gone through the refiner's fire, and that fire will continue to refine us time after time after time until we go to Heaven. And time after time, God is calling you and me out and will continue to call us out and say all the wonderful things we are doing. He wants you to always remember Him. He is the reason you have life, both physically and spiritually, and He will call out our sin because He wants all of us and all of our sins. Christ already took our sin, now He wants all of us.

Like Ephesus, do not look at the reward Christ has for you. As you come out of the storm, consider the areas of your life that still need refining, that you need to confess and repent.

Beauty awaits us beyond this life. Let us press onward and conquer in this life that we may taste and see the goodness of the Lord in the glorious life to come.

51

Reflections for the Ages

"My son, beware of anything beyond these. Of making many books there is no end, and much study is a weariness of the flesh. The end of the matter: all has been heard. Fear God and keep his commandments, for this is the whole duty of man. For God will bring every deed into judgment, with every secret thing, whether good or evil."

~ Ecclesiastes 12:12-14

The end of trials or seasons of life allows us to reflect on where we have been. Depending upon our age, we can look back on years and decades. Solomon, at the end of Ecclesiastes, is looking back on a life of loss, a life that was not well-lived. As he looks to the past, he realizes he has made so many mistakes; he has disobeyed the Lord and lived in sin the majority of his life. In these latter days of his life on earth he wants to leave us with some wisdom. In 1 Kings 4:30, it is said, "that Solomon's wisdom surpassed the wisdom of all the people of the east and all the wisdom of Egypt." The wisest man in the known world wants to leave us with some wisdom, not from the world, but from the Lord. His words were that were poignant in his day and are just as poignant, if not more, in our day.

He leaves us with two pieces of wisdom from these verses that hopefully we can learn now and not a lifetime later as Solomon did. He says, "Fear God" and "Keep His commandments." Everything in our lives comes down to our relationship with the Lord. Are we willing to put God above everything in our lives? Are we going to understand our relationship with the Lord and live according to the way He wants in faithfulness and righteousness?

Solomon was the wisest man who ever lived. In the New Testament, Jesus' words regarding life, salvation, wisdom—everything—trumps any wisdom that was ever said or thought. In response to a question the Jewish leaders posed to Jesus regarding the greatest commandment, He replies in Matthew 22:37-40, "You shall love the Lord your God with all your heart and with all your soul and with all your mind. This is the great and first commandment. And a second is like it: You shall love your neighbor as yourself. On these two commandments depend all the Law and the Prophets." Jesus just summed up the entire Old Testament, and in that statement, the entirety of how the Lord wants us to live.

The first is to love the Lord with everything you are, literally everything; every thought, every word, and every action lived out in love for Christ. It is an incredible summation of the commandments because if we love God, we will do what He says and live as He wants.

The second is an outward manifestation of our love for God. We are to direct this love towards our neighbors, men and women who need Christ, who are created in the image of God. We live in a world where rather than helping each other, we help ourselves; thinking ourselves the mighty Trinity (the almighty me, myself, and I). In this second command, what stands out is that our focus is not on us, but others. If we learned anything from Adam and Eve, we learned that when we love ourselves over the Lord it never works out for anyone's good, and Jesus is bringing us back to that moment and turning the tide of life and sin, as He will do on the cross, to focus on God and our neighbor. As humans we tend to fight for our own good, and now, in Christ, we are to fight for the good of our neighbor, to love them as God loves them.

We have been given this time to rethink our relationship with the Lord, to fear Him, to love Him, to live for Him, and to love His creation and those made in His image, meaning everyone.

52

Rejoice and Rest

"Not only that, but we rejoice in our sufferings, knowing that suffering produces endurance, and endurance produces character, and character produces hope, and hope does not put us to shame, because God's love has been poured into our hearts through the Holy Spirit who has been given to us."

~ Romans 5:3-5

Every work of the hand of God has a purpose to it. Not one thing happens in our lives as Christ-followers without the Lord having a purpose in it. It is hard to believe sometimes that one event, one interaction, one conversation, one diagnosis is so bad that it lacks purpose. But remember that we are in Christ, and there is purpose in every part of our lives. There is always something to learn, something to confess, something to refine, something to share. Our stories and events of our lives all have meaning, they have a reason.

The verses above were used earlier in this book and we have seen the many things that our suffering brings, and amongst the pain so many incredible things produced through our trial. For this entry, consider a part of the verse, "we rejoice in our sufferings," and in that short part, consider the word "rejoice." Paul calls us to rejoice in our sufferings, and subsequently "rejoice" in the calm. As life calms down for a few moments before the next storm, we can reflect on how God has worked in our lives, remembering the hand of God in our suffering and praising Him for His presence.

The qualities of life that come out of suffering are not qualities that we will master in the storm or the calm, they are qualities we will be working on until we go to Heaven. Still, we can look back at the difficult days we have faced and see how we have grown in those areas and grown closer to the Lord.

In God granting us time to work on ourselves and our relationship with Him, we can rejoice. We can look back during this time of rest, remember the pain and remember the goodness of the Lord. In the storm and in the calm, we can say what Paul says to the Philippians in verse 4:4, "Rejoice in the Lord always; again I say rejoice."

53

A Call Opposed

"But you are a chosen race, a royal priesthood, a holy nation, a people for his own possession, that you may proclaim the excellencies of him who called you out of darkness into his marvelous light."

~ I Peter 2:9

God has a great love for His creation. He loves the earth, the animals, and most of all, the people created in His own image, mankind as a whole. Despite our sin, God loves each one of us. Yes, God loves His creation, but He has an even greater love for His children. As a Christ-follower, you are a child of God, belonging to the family of God. Imagine that! You possess a special status in this world as a child of God. The world and unbelievers have no idea of the special status you hold, but God does. Peter describes in verse 9 that as a Christian, "you are a chosen race, a holy nation, a people of his own possession." You belong to a completely different race this world does not even have a clue about or has ever seen. It is not just a nation, but a kingdom. You belong to a nation that presently has no name in this world, a nation unnamed save for its leader, God Almighty. You are a person of His possession, sealed and secured by the Spirit. You belong to Him, not as just a member of a special club, but a member of His family.

Peter contrasts your present role in Christ with the role you held as a sinner, an enemy of God. The word "enemy" is a harsh word for those who do not believe in Christ as their Savior, but it is an accurate word for those who have absolutely no interest in knowing Him and want nothing to do with Him, who look at Him as the enemy. Yet, verse 10 says, "once you were not a people." God does not consider His enemies a people, other than as enemies. Peter continues in verse 10, "But now you are God's people; once you had not received mercy, but now you have received mercy." Once you were an enemy, now you are family. The Lord has looked at you, called you to salvation, given you mercy, and made you a part of His family. You are a member of His family, but presently you live in a world with absolutely no interest in the Bible, in salvation, or in Christ.

Consider, for example, a discussion on religion. In our society, we can talk about any religion: Judaism, Buddhism, Islam, even cults, and no one bats an eye to the discussion. You can even talk about "god," and the discussion continues. But when Christ's name is presented in the discussion, the discussion becomes hostile and maybe even abruptly ends.

You live in a world hostile to Christ and maybe hostile to you. If you haven't experienced this hostility, some day you will. Christ has a special role for you in His kingdom. On this earth, you also have a special role, the role of "alien." As aliens, our lives should be lived differently in every way, in a way that brings attention to Christ, that others may be saved, and Christ may be glorified through you. *Anchored to the Son* is a book about moving to a new perspective in this life, realizing that we truly do not fit into this world.

Peter finishes this passage to "aliens" writing, "Beloved, I urge you as sojourners and exiles to abstain from the passions of the flesh, which wage war against your soul. Keep your conduct among the Gentiles honorable, so that when they speak against you as evil-doers, they may see your good deeds and glorify God on the day of visitation" (1 Peter 2:11-12).

Most likely, you have led a journey through suffering to get to this point. This side of Heaven, we live a life of suffering, knowing the Lord has better things ahead for us in heaven. While we are here on this earth, we are expected to have good conduct among unbelievers, so that when they accuse us of doing evil, there is nothing true about their claims. It is interesting that in the 21st century, we see what was once evil is now good, and what was once good is now evil. It always relates to Christians and what the Lord has called us to do and be in this world. Your testimony will stand against any false accusations whether an unbelieving world agrees or disagrees.

God's calling on your life is not the world's calling. You are His possession, called to Him for His purpose, to explain to the world Him "who has called you out of darkness into his marvelous light" (1 Peter 2:9). He is that marvelous light, and He is calling you unto Himself.

Be an alien in this world and be at home in Christ!

54

Seen and Heard

"For you will be a witness for him to everyone of what you have seen and heard."

~ **Acts 22:15**

I have entered the age where my high school experience is completely different than the high school students I teach in my classroom. I often say to them, to their chagrin, of course, "When I was a kid, we wrestled bears outdoors for fun. We chewed coffee beans like real men instead of drinking it frothy and sugary and ate dirt when we didn't have any food."

Are you that old yet? One of the things I enjoy about teaching history as I've gotten older is to be able to discuss with students the history I have experienced. The horror of 9/11 stands utmost in my mind, but also the Challenger, the 1984 Olympics, Reagan declaring "Mr. Gorbachev, tear down this wall!" And do I dare say being riveted to the TV watching the OJ Simpson white Bronco chase. Those were events that I saw and experienced, I am sure you remember others I did not. Some changed our world drastically, and others are just conversation topics, "Where were you when _____?"

Think back what the pillars of biblical history would have to say from Abraham and Sarah to Moses, to Joshua, to Esther, to Elijah, all the prophets, the disciples, and the early church. All saw God at work in ways they could never have imagined. Their experiences, particularly with God, were out of the ordinary. Only ones you and I can dream. These pillars were uniquely chosen for a specific purpose to display God's power and glory in the Bible and to the world. You and I are in many ways chosen for a different part of the biblical story; one we will see in Heaven. And just as the biblical leaders saw God work in extraordinary circumstances, so you and I are firsthand witnesses to God's work in our lives, our families, our friends, and our churches.

While I was going through cancer, I saw time and time again God's hand upon my circumstances. He orchestrated events in ways that led to treatment, healing, and these two *Anchored* books. God did not work in my life like He took Elijah to glory on a fiery chariot, or defeat my enemies as He did through Moses to the Egyptians. God worked more quietly, subtly, but one thing I have realized in my life is that sometimes the quietest, most subtle experiences can be the most impacting in our lives. I may not re-member each quiet moment where God worked, but I knew God was present and working. There was a purpose beyond myself in it. God was at work, not just in my life, but also in my family, friends, colleagues, and church. It was extraordinary! And it continues to be!

As I left cancer behind in 2015 and moved towards healing and understanding of my cancer, a verse stuck out in the last chapter of Job. In Job 42:5, Job says "I heard of you by the hearing of [my] ear, but now my eye sees you." God had always been so faithful over the years, seemingly present in so many ways, but cancer took our relationship to a deeper level. It was not something I did, though I did reach out in prayer. It was His work, His presence in my life. In these moments, like Job, I knew God, but now I really know God, in ways I had ever known Him before. His work in and through my cancer and suffering is astonishing. And as I headed into 2015, I understood Job, "I heard of you by the hearing of [my] ear, but now my eye sees you." God had worked wonders I never fully understood, and even now that verse astounds me as I understand God more deeply, and intimately than I ever had before.

Your suffering and now your time out of the storm is an incredible opportunity for you to see God at work in and through you and your circumstances. You are a witness to God's work. Witnesses speak truth about what you have seen and heard.

55

More and Less

"I know how to be brought low, and I know how to abound. In any and every circumstance, I have learned the secret of facing plenty and hunger, abundance and need. I can do all things through him who strengthens me."

~ **Philippians 4:12-13**

---

o you ever take time to look back at life and compare and contrast it to today? I admit that recently I have been on a kick looking at life in the 1980s, particularly the things I enjoyed as a kid. I was born in 1981 and look with great fondness at the joys of being a child during this time period. It was a significant decade in our country's history, especially as the last decade of the Cold War. America was in many ways at its pinnacle of power. But there were dark days in the 80s, into the 90s, the 2000s, all the way to the present. In life it always seems the easy is always mixed with the hard.

Paul knows the ease and comfort of life and the difficult and arduous times of suffering. For Paul, it is such a stark contrast, and no doubt his mind is rushing with various memories, some delightful, but others so horrendous. Paul, a Pharisee of Pharisees, lived a life of wealth, privilege, education, and power. Paul had the life that very few have and many of us envy, a life of seemingly everything a person could ever want. There was a dark side to Paul, though.

He held such influence that he was one who targeted Christians for persecution and execution. According to the culture at the time, he was doing everything well and was on the path to great success. What a terrible thing to consider his great success was in killing people, or at least allowing people to be killed under his watch.

But Paul, as the author of Philippians, is now completely different. The Lord had called him to salvation in a mighty way. From Christian killer to Christian proclaimer, Paul gave up everything to follow Christ. He chose a life of suffering over a life of ease. When He talks of "plenty and hunger ... abundance and need," he talks from personal experience. As a follower of Jesus Christ, Paul's life was most of all a life of hunger and need. While traveling around the Roman Empire, he did not live at the church's expense, but his own. He left the comforts of life to trust in Jesus Christ, our Lord. I will let Paul describe the sufferings of his life in 2 Corinthians 11:24-28. He says, "Five times I received at the hands of the Jews the forty lashes less one. Three times I was beaten with rods. Once I was stoned. Three times I was shipwrecked; a night and a day I was adrift at sea; on frequent journeys, in danger from rivers, danger from robbers, danger from my own people, danger from Gentiles, danger in the city, danger in the wilderness, danger at sea, danger from false brothers; in toil and hardship, through many a sleepless night, in hunger and thirst, often without food, in cold and exposure. And apart from other things, there is the daily pressure on me of my anxiety for all the church."

Most likely, you and I will not face trials as Paul did. That is not to say what we have suffered is not meaningless. For Paul, and most likely us, before we came to Christ, life was easy, almost carefree, but our trials seem to increase since we came to Christ. I pray that Paul's life is an encouragement to you. Throughout all of his suffering, Paul would say it was a joy to suffer for Christ, and if he had the choice, he would do it all over again if it meant Christ was preached before an unbelieving world.

Like Paul, you now have your testimony to show that you have seen Christ at work in the calm and in the storm. You know "how to abound" and "how to be brought low." You know the light and the dark, the calm and the storm. This makes you just like Paul who through God, you can do all things according to His will. Paul's storm never ended this side of Heaven, as yours might not either, but Paul's attitude towards the gospel always remained that God was going to do great things through him. God is doing to do great things through those who are fully equipped and consecrated to Him.

And yes, "[you] can do all things *through Him* who strengthens [you]." (emphasis mine)

56

Fulfilled

"The Spirit of the Lord God is upon me, because the Lord has anointed me to bring good news to the poor; he has sent me to bind up the brokenhearted, to proclaim liberty to the captives, and the opening of the prison to those who are bound."

~ Isaiah 61:1

After 30 years of life, Jesus came to the synagogue in Nazareth to begin his three-year ministry to change the world to bring salvation and a ministry that continues to impact this world and saves lives even at the moment of this reading. He came to fulfill what the Lord had tasked Him with before the dawn of creation, the salvation of mankind. The first words He says starting his ministry was prophesied by Isaiah. At this moment, before many attendees, he knew personally for years, Jesus declares Himself Messiah. This is the moment where the Messiah is here, is real, is going to act in a way, not to save a nation, but to save the world.

In Luke 4:17-21 Luke writes "And the scroll of the prophet Isaiah was given to him. He unrolled the scroll and found the place where it was written, 'The Spirit of the Lord is upon me, because he has anointed me to proclaim good news to the poor. He has sent me to proclaim liberty to the captives and recovering of sight to the blind, to set at liberty those who are oppressed, to proclaim the year of the Lord's favor.' And he rolled up the scroll and gave it back to the attendant and sat down. And the eyes of all in the synagogue were fixed on him. And he began to say to them, 'Today this Scripture has been fulfilled in your hearing.'"

In declaring Himself Messiah, Jesus states four things that are going to happen because He is here. The first is "good news to the poor." The poor can be a specific group of people who are economically or physically poor. Still, the poor can also be spiritually poor people. Both are important groups and have their needs. Christ's abundant grace in providing us the opportunity for salvation fulfills any needs of the spiritually poor. There is a reason we call the gospel the "good news".

The next proclamation is "liberty to the captives." Who are the captives? Going back to the poor, recall that all mankind is imprisoned to sin. We are born in sin, live in sin, and without Christ we will die in sin, suffering an eternity of torment because of our sin. We were captive, burdened, bound, and incapable of freedom, but Christ comes and declares "LIBERTY!!!" He provides freedom from what has held us captive: sin. Our world thinks that sin is freedom, choosing to do what makes us happy, makes us feel good, the freedom to choose any path that the almighty "Me" wants to do. But what we call "freedom" in our world is truly imprisonment. We are born imprisoned, there is no doubt about it, but Christ is here to free the captives, so we can be liberated and free to choose NOT to sin. It is an extraordinary reality that I think so few of us consider and dwell on. You are free from sin, free from choosing to sin. In Christ, you are not captive to anything, but you are held in the gracious arms of a Father who loves you and would do anything for you, including taking your sin and placing it on His Son, all for you!

The third thing proclaimed in the synagogue is making the blind see. As we know from the gospels, there are several instances where Jesus works a miracle for several blind people. In our case, most of us are not physically blind, but like the paragraphs above, we are blind to our sin; we are blind that we act against a God who is love. Jesus is going to open the eyes of the world to who He is and why He is here. The choice is there, you can accept Him as Lord and Savior and receive all that goes along with being a child of God through faith in Christ. Or you can continue in blindness and deny Jesus as your Lord and Savior and choose an eternity in hell aware of the truth of Christ, but not in the presence of Christ.

The last proclamation of the year is of the Lord's favor. The Lord is present in our world; this world is forever changed, and the blessing of salvation is now proclaimed. The mysteries of the Messiah are answered. This is the year of the Lord, continuing until the day our sin-filled world and Christ-followers are brought into His presence for all eternity.

After reading the scroll, Jesus hands it back to the synagogue attendee and takes a seat amongst the congregation. The crowds' eyes have been riveted on Him during this short declaration, and their eyes are on Him as He states, "Today this Scripture has been fulfilled in your hearing." While all eyes are on Him, there was dead silence, all mouths open with nothing to say, no way to respond. There is something about Jesus that draws people's attention, and here He is declaring who He is and what He is going to do.

In this one moment of Jesus starting a ministry, you too have been given time to start your ministry, you sharing God's story through you, to the world. You have seen God work in wondrous ways through your suffering, and He has gifted you time to reflect and pray over where you go from here. Your ministry is not going to be like Jesus'. He is Jesus, but consider what God has before you in ministry. As a follower of Jesus Christ, He is not going to waste one moment of your life for His kingdom; everything has a purpose.

What is God calling you to do? How is God going to use you for His kingdom?

57

King of Glory

"Who shall ascend the hill of the Lord?
And who shall stand in his holy place?"

~ Psalm 24:3

———•———

Consider the reality of the Lord. The psalmist writes that he is on a hill, a mountaintop, asking, "Who shall ascend the hill of the Lord?" Who can come to God? Take a moment and consider the religions of this world besides biblical Christianity. In all those religions, how does one access their god? Consider what it takes for "salvation" in other religions. Other religions say you need to do this and do that, give this and give that, visit this and visit that, pay this and pay that. There is a long list of the works one needs to accomplish. At the end of life, there is the assurance of salvation. How is one to know if one is good enough or done enough to be saved? There is no guarantee.

But what do we know about our God? In the Garden, God walked with Adam and Eve before they sinned. Abraham talked with God and trusted God's promise of creating a people more numerous than the stars. Moses talked with God on Mount Sinai, delivering the Ten Commandments of God to the people of Israel and the world. Even though the sin of mankind taints this world, He continues to reach out to His people. The prophets represent

God's will and desire for the people of Israel. It is not until the birth of Jesus that God reenters this world to live and spread His message of salvation, to die for a people who have chosen disobedience, to raise Himself from the dead, and to ascend to heaven.

What does this say about God in contrast with the other religions?

From Genesis to Revelation, God is seeking relationship with His creation, the people of His hand and of His image. He steps away from His throne, "the hill of the Lord," for the sake of His people. Who leaves such splendor for those who want nothing to do with them? Jesus does.

Unlike the other religions where man has to reach out to their god, Jesus reaches to a world that is hostile to Him doing what is necessary to bring salvation to those who desire salvation. Paul writes in Acts 4:12, "And there is salvation in no one else, for there is no other name under heaven given among men by which we must be saved." Through Christ alone is the hope for mankind.

Now remember David says "Who shall ascend the hill of the Lord? And who shall stand in his holy place?" Those who are called by God to believe in God are those who can ascend because God has already descended and created a way through Him for them to ascend to this holy place where God resides.

As Christ-followers, we do not need to work our way towards God, but we have the answer to the world's question, "Who is the King of glory?" It is "The Lord of hosts, he is the King of glory!" (Psalm 24:10). And this King of glory has come down from His mount to save mankind!

58

Delight in the Lord

"Trust in the Lord, and do good, dwell in the land and befriend faithfulness. Delight yourself in the Lord, and he will give you the desire of your heart. Commit your ways to the Lord; trust in him and he will act. He will bring forth your righteousness as the light, and your justice as the noonday. Be still before the Lord and wait patiently for him; fret not yourself over the one who prospers in his way, over the man who carries out evil deeds."

~ Psalm 37:3-7

For years, these verses sat in a frame on my bookcase, right where I place my keys, wallet, glasses, and other items from my pockets. This verse has been one of my favorites for many years, and it allowed me to see that in every part of life, it all comes to down to the Lord and how I embrace the Lord's will and work in and through me.

David continues to encourage our hearts in the calm through his passages. Remember, David is just like you and me. The Lord had special plans for David far beyond the impact ours will be, but know the Lord's plans for you are also to declare Himself through our lives, that we may live lives worthy of his calling for the sake of sharing the gospel in a world in need.

Several things stand out in this brief but significant passage. In the last line in verse 7 it says, "fret not yourself over the one who prospers in his way, over the man who carries out evil deeds." Our world is full of many contradictions. Those who do good tend to suffer, and those who do evil tend to prosper. Even many unbelievers feel that something is wrong when the evil prosper. It almost goes against who we are.

Sadly, sin still reigns in this world and will reign until Christ's return. The key to the passage is not that the evil prosper and the good suffer. It is that we should not fret ourselves over it. As believers, we know God is working. A widely accepted theme of the Christian life is Romans 8:28, "And we know that for those who love God all things work together for good, for those who are called according to his purpose." You are a follower of Christ, and as a follower of Christ, you trust that all things are going to work out for your favor. It is not going to happen in the fullness of today, tomorrow, or far into the future until we are in the presence of God.

As David reminds us not to fret, he writes about how we can react to a world where all seems to be going upside down. He gives several exhortations to those who belong to the Lord. Let us see what we can take away as we try and understand our place in this broken world.

The first is "Trust in the Lord, and do good" (Psalm 37:3). We are called to look out for one another. God does not specify we should care exclusively for other believers, but in doing good in this world, our work will be noticed by others. People will wonder and inquire as to why we even care about another human being. Jesus says in John 13:35, "By this, all people will know that you are my disciples, if you have love for one another." God is going to work in our lives, and we need to trust Him through the easy and difficult paths of our lives. While we are traversing these paths, we need to care for those around us in kind words, kind deeds, and displays of authentic care and concern for others. Remember the sinner and the saint were all made in the image of God. Trust in God and act as He acts!

The second is "Delight yourself in the Lord" (Psalm 37:4). I focus on the first part of the verse because it is probably the hardest thing for us to do at any moment in our lives, no matter how good or how bad things are. We know that God is going to work in every part of our lives, so instead of focusing on those particular moments, think of the Lord and delight in what He is doing through your life. Delight that He has worked in your life, both the good and the bad. And He will continue to work in your life for all eternity.

I admit that in looking at the second part of the verse, "he will give you the desire of your heart" was the priority of my life. I put my desires above Him. I would want one particular thing or want a particular outcome of a meeting. But I was wrong because God is primary and when I put God in His rightful place, all things work out. I am not sure if harmony is the right word, but when God and I are on the same page everything works; my heart's desires are what He wants because I want what He wants. It is an absolutely beautiful reality when we live in perfect union with the Lord. When His plans are above ours the desire of our heart is Him and what He wants.

The third is "Commit your way to the Lord" (Psalm 37:5). You know that life has its twists and turns. It is expected, and as we have seen in our trials, unexpected. Our way before the Lord is not "our" way, but it is His way. I distinctly remember the day I had one of my brain surgeries that I felt an intense calm. I did not know what would happen during surgery; I did not know the outcome or possible lingering effects or disabilities, but I knew the Lord was with me, the doctor and his team, and those in the waiting room. Before I even went into the surgery room, I knew that God was already there, and I knew that God was already on the other side of the surgery. Whatever the outcome, He was there.

It was quite an experience. I had never had surgery before, except my wisdom teeth. I knew nothing of what I was facing, but I knew a God who did. I knew a God who knew what problems I might face after surgery. I knew God would be at work in the life ahead.

These are the words that were upon my heart. It was a tremendous gift from the Lord to pray, "God, I don't know what you're doing. I don't know what the future holds, whether I will live or not, but I do know You Lord, and I know You are going to act according to Your will and purpose. I trust the outcome is what You desire." And we know from the rest of the verse God is going to act. God is going to work out your righteousness and your justice.

And here we are again. Because of the Lord, you will prosper in your life. Life is not about material prosperity, it is about knowing the Lord, and in our suffering, we have seen God work. In our calm, we are continuing that relationship with the Lord. We are trusting in Him, allowing Him to work, processing what we have been through so we can continue on our journey of knowing Christ better and becoming more like Him.

As we take on life again and the mysteries of what the Lord has in store for us, we are left with a beautiful place to stand in verse 7, "Be still before the Lord and wait patiently for him."

59

A Place, a Name

*""For thus says the Lord: To the eunuchs who keep my Sabbaths, who
choose the things that please me and hold fast my covenant, I will
give in my house and within my walls a monument and a name
better than sons and daughters; I will give them an everlasting
name that shall not be cut off."*

~ Isaiah 56:4-5

———◆———

Just days into creation, God's creation realized something --
Adam, in particular, realizes something—he is alone. Adam
was literally given everything in the Garden, the earth itself.
He was a caretaker, guide, the leader of this beautiful earth
Lord created. Adam was tasked with naming the animals: "The
man gave names to all livestock and to the birds of the heavens
and to every beast of the field" (Genesis 2:20a). We can imagine
the animals walking or flying by as Adam names them, two by
two they came. As they pass by, Adam notices the animals in pairs,
"But for Adam there was not found a helper fit for him" (Genesis 2:20b). He is looking at these incredible creatures walking,
trotting, almost bowing to Adam as they walk by, and Adam is
wondering what his place in this world is. The male elephant has
a female elephant. The male pelican has a female pelican, yet there
is Adam and just Adam. This was a place made for him, and it was
just him—alone.

Our world can be a very lonely place, even our churches can
be lonely. It is surprising how lonely life can be despite the use of

our phones and social media and the "connection" we have with hundreds if not thousands of "friends." We seem more connected to people now than ever before, but the reality is loneliness is more a plague now than ever before in human history. In that loneliness, suicide is a horrific affliction in our western countries. God understands our loneliness, just as He understood Adam's loneliness. God created Eve for Adam, as a woman needs a man, and a man needs a woman. There are people in our churches and in our world who, for one reason or another, find themselves alone. They could be in a relationship that is broken and nonexistent, a relationship that was separated by death, or even a relationship that never was. Loneliness seems to be something mankind has faced from the dawn of time, yet God always comes eager to know and to be intimately involved with His creation.

What amazes me about God is how He works through all parts of our lives, and whether we were lonely during our trials or are lonely right now, God is working. Several years ago, I heard this verse from a sermon, and it has stuck with me as an incredible verse for the lonely. In Isaiah 56:4-5 it says, "For thus says the Lord: 'To the eunuchs who keep my Sabbaths, who choose the things that please me and hold fast my covenant, I will give in my house and within my walls a monument and a name better than sons and daughters; I will give them an everlasting name that shall not be cut off.'" Go back and reread it. God is talking about this group of people, eunuchs in particular, who may face an entire life of loneliness and a life unlike many of their peers, particularly in the church.

Now I have to say there are a couple of caveats to the verses. The first is it comes from a historical context that we may not completely understand today. As far as I know, we do not have any group of people who are eunuchs, men who have been physically emasculated. However, we do have many men and women who are for a variety of reasons still single into their upper ages, who because of their singleness will not be married and will not have children of their own.

What stood out to me, and actually made me excited about these verses as an unmarried man, was how God interacts with this unique group. We can see throughout the Bible that God literally adores His people. He knows them, loves them, and is willing to do absolutely anything for them. Remember, Jesus died for you. Clearly, He would do anything for His family. There is not anything God would not do for His people. What God has planned for those who are in this group is just so special. God is calling out this group, these "uniques," who have been faithful and obedient to the Lord. They have loved the Lord, and realize their situation of being alone in the world, but better understand their position in the kingdom than many others. He says, "I will give in my house and within my walls a monument and a name better than sons and daughters; I will give them an everlasting name that shall not be cut off."

There is so much in that verse. The first thing that stood out was God saying to this unique group, "in my house … within my walls," meaning that we as Christ-followers will live within the place where God dwells. This is for all of us. I have prayed many times since cancer to see a brief glimpse of Heaven, a place where you and I will be in eternity. To be present with God in Heaven is just out of this world, something no one can even come close to comprehending. Words cannot describe this place, and the wonderful thing for us is that we will be there with God, together for eternity!

Within the walls of Heaven, God's dwelling place is a monument for those who make sacrifices so they may pursue the Lord. It is a monument, a place of honor, a place of thought and contemplation, a place of worshipping the Lord in all parts of life. As I mentioned earlier, the eunuchs of the past or never-married of the present, are rarely choosing their singleness. Most times it is out of their hands, but it's how they choose to embrace God's work in their lives that sets them apart from others who just want to get married. They are willing to put aside so many parts of life on this earth for the sake of the Lord that the Lord has a special place in Heaven, just for them.

For the eunuch or the never-married in Christ, the reality is there are no children, the family name literally dies with you. You are the end of the line. It is a tough truth to face when you are in this position because, however long this world continues, there will not be someone to carry the family, to carry your story, to bear your history into future generations. It stuns me what God does for this group. He says, "I will give them an everlasting name that shall not be cut off" (Isaiah 56:5b). What an incredible honor is given to those who put aside so very much for the Lord's work on this earth and in this life. An everlasting name, a name that continues on that does not end and is not cut off for the rest of forever.

I am sure you are thinking, "What does this mean for us who are lonely yet have not chosen such specific things as lifelong singleness? What do these verses matter to me at any part of life, lonely or not?" I get it that these two verses out of thousands in the Bible might be an encouragement to a tiny, even minuscule group within the Lord's church. But what do we learn about God in these verses? I am going to ask you three questions:

Is there any one of God's children that he does not care about? Think about for a moment. In our churches we have naturally grouped off, separating ourselves based upon who we are and our status in the world. People can come to Sunday service, sit down, not be greeted by someone, be in the service, leave after service, not having interacted with a single person, and yet met God and heard God's word. We may not connect with each person we meet at church, but God does connect and cares deeply about each of us. He cares about you, your relationship with Him, and with others. God loves and cares for you just as much as the eunuchs.

Is God's home your home? We get an incredible and momentary glimpse of two things in Heaven in this passage. For all Christ-followers, Heaven is home. God has made a place for you in His home. Think about it. There is a place in Heaven that has your name on it. God has taken the time to prepare, to craft a place just for you. And as we all look toward Heaven as a place we will one day enter, there is a place in Heaven that will be yours in a place that's God's, a place designed uniquely as you in the home of God.

A special name is given to this unique group, and you may be thinking, "What about my name? Don't I get a special name?" In this third question, we cannot assume that everything revealed in the scriptures is everything that is ever going to be revealed. We cannot assume that this group is the only group that gets a special name. God has only chosen to reveal that those in this position will have an everlasting name, a name that continues.

If you have children, your name continues into the future. If you chose singleness and have no children, the family name that has gone throughout history, all the way back to Adam and Eve, is gone. It truly is a significant sacrifice for the good of the Lord. Peter gives us a great reminder when it comes to God-honoring each of His children: "And when the chief Shepherd appears, you will receive the unfading crown of glory" (1 Peter 5:4). God is going to honor each of us, despite our sin, despite our disobedience even as His children. God is going to rewards us, as undeserving as we are, but He is going to have the biggest smile on His face as that crown of glory is placed on our heads.

For our time in the calm, and in the storm, we can look ahead to Heaven, to what God has promised as His children and Him creating a place for us. The hope is not in our status in this world; the hope is in our status in Christ. Whether single, divorced, widowed, whatever our status is on this earth, in Christ we are all God's children, and we bear His name and will one day live with Him in the place prepared for us by Him.

Wherever we stand in this life, relish where you stand in the next life with Christ ... forever!

60

If I Perish, I Perish

"Then Esther told them to reply to Mordecai, 'Go, gather all the Jews to be found in Susa, and hold a fast on my behalf, and do not eat or drink for three days, night or day, I and my young women will also fast as you do. Then I will go to the king, though it is against the law, and if I perish, I perish.'"

~ Esther 4:15-16

Just look around, and you will see that our world, our country, and our people are changing fast. What was once good is now evil, and what was evil is now good! Our world is changing quicker than we can ever imagine, and it is just going to change faster and faster and faster, and a huge part of the change is in the world turning away from anything related in any way to Christ and Christianity. At some point in the future, even our future, because we are in Christ, we will be targeted, persecuted, possibly imprisoned and executed, all for our belief that Jesus Christ is our Savior. It is coming, either in our lifetime or the generations to come.

When the time of persecution comes, when everything you live for and stand for is put on the line, how will you react? When it is all on the line for the sake of Christ, what will your response be? Christ or your life?

Esther, the book's namesake, is the queen of Persia. Being queen in Persia does not hold any political power. Even as the king's wife, she has minimal power, if any personally, with the king. He calls, she goes. It can be a precarious situation for her. As queen, she is told of a plot to destroy and exterminate the entirety of the Jewish population within the Persian empire. She is Jewish; she is part of God's chosen people. With her people and herself facing extermination, she has to make a choice. She could be silent and allow the execution order to go through; she can stay and enjoy the privilege as a royal. She may be found out as a Jew and thus executed for being Jewish even though she is queen. Or she can stand up and stand out, go to the king, appeal for the lives of the Jews and herself. As she tells her uncle Mordecai before entering the throne room, "If I perish, I perish." She was willing to say goodbye to everything for the sake of her people.

Esther sacrifices herself, her dreams, her life as queen for the sake of her people—God's people. Would those be words you could ever say? If you knew our government was targeting Christians and you stood before a police officer, or a raucous crowd, all calling for your execution, what would you say in that situation?

During this time of calm, it is important to consider your standing in Christ. I pray we do not face these times, that the Lord takes us home before these troubling times come. But if they do, what would you say? Could you stand and say with Esther, "If I perish, I perish"?

61

Eighteen Songs*

> *"Oh sing to the Lord a new song, for he has done marvelous things! His right hand and his holy arm have worked salvation for him. The Lord has made known his salvation; he has revealed his righteousness in the sight of the nations ... Make a joyful noise to the Lord, all the earth; break forth into joyous song and sing praises! ... Let the sea roar, and all that fills it; the world and those who dwell in it!"*
>
> ~ Esther 4:15-16

Music has a way of expressing human emotion in a completely different way than any words ever could. It has a way of taking our innermost thoughts and bringing them to light. The fourteen songs in *Anchored in the Storm* defined a trial for me, and I pray they were encouraging to you too. The eighteen songs of *Anchored to the Son* are songs that have touched me at no particular time of life, but in many moments throughout life and seem to fit appropriately when our trials are over, as we learn to live a life of a new normal and a new perspective.

These eighteen songs I pray will be an encouragement and inspiration to you. They draw me to the Lord in the storm and the calm. As we come out of our storms, I pray that we can continue to grow closer and stronger to the Lord and that these songs are ones that strengthen your relationship with the Lord. The road of this life is still long, and our songs and prayers can continue to go up to the Lord as a fragrant offering of our praise for what He has done in our lives.

I have intentionally left most of the lyrics out of the entries so that you may listen to each song as the artist intended. All are easily accessible on the Internet. Hopefully, you have already heard some of the songs before or have even sung them in your church or, as I do, in my car.

I pray as you listen to these songs and read a short commentary, that you will have a new song in the new normal of your life. Christ may have worked so drastically in your life that a song may stand out to you as a new anthem in your relationship with Him, and I pray that is the case for each reader.

He has done such incredible things that I pray Moses' words in Deuteronomy 10:21 will be a new hymn of a life refreshed by the Almighty: "He is your praise. He is your God, who has done for you these great and terrifying things that your eyes have seen."

*Adapted from *Anchored in the Storm*

62

"Carried to the Table"

"So Mephibosheth lived in Jerusalem, for he ate always at the king's table. Now he was lame in both his feet."

~ 2 Samuel 9:13

"Carried to the Table" by Leeland

———◆———

This song is one that tears my heartstrings in many ways. When I first heard this song and its album "Sound of Melodies," a family friend was dying of cancer. From the song, I understood this sick and weakening man was on his way to the table of the Lord, a place of restoration, absolute renewal; he was on his way to an eternal place in the presence of the Lord. Later I realized that I was partly right, but the band took inspiration from a man in the Old Testament, Mephibosheth. Do you remember him?

Early on in David's service to King Saul, David and Saul's son Jonathan, were best friends, so much so that in 1 Samuel 18:3 it says, "Then Jonathan made a covenant with David, because he loved him as his own soul." David and Jonathan's closeness is nothing we see in most friendships today. The commitment and loyalty they had together is so rare amongst even the church. Jonathan knew of the Lord's promise to Israel that David would be the next king after Saul, an interesting place for Jonathan because Jonathan was next in line as Saul's son. If you know anything of Saul, you know he is jealous of David's success, and his future, and that the Lord's hand is upon him. Jonathan sought to honor the Lord, and in 1 Samuel 23:17, Jonathan tells David, "Do not fear, for the hand of Saul my father shall not find you. You shall be king over Israel, and I shall be next to you. Saul my father also knows this." It would be hard for anyone who is guaranteed a place of power and position by blood to give up their rightful place on the throne. Jonathan does not just guarantee his support of David as the next king but will stand beside him as a helper and servant.

But Jonathan would not see David taking the place of the king. At the end of 1 Samuel, we learn that in 1 Samuel 31:6, "Thus Saul died, and his three sons, and his armor-bearer, and all his men on the same day together." You could say there was no one to take up the banner of Saul's family and reign. All were gone.

The loss of Jonathan is one of the hardest times of David's life. Saul had threatened him throughout 1 Samuel, but David understood his role in Saul's kingdom and mourned Saul, Jonathan, and the entire family. David was reflecting upon his promise to Jonathan and the house of Saul. Twice David has promised not to wipe out the house of Saul and Jonathan. First in 1 Samuel 20:42, "Then Jonathan said to David, 'Go in peace, because we have sworn both of us in the name of the Lord, saying, 'The Lord shall be between me and you, and between my offspring and your offspring, forever.'" And David expresses this covenant of Jonathan and David to Saul just chapters later in 1 Samuel 24:18-22: "And you have declared this day how you have dealt well with me; in that you did not kill me when the Lord put me in your hands. For if a man finds his enemy, will he let him go away safe? So may the Lord reward you with good for what you have done to me this day. And now, behold, I know that you shall surely be king, and that the kingdom of Israel shall be stabled in your hand. Swear to me, therefore by the Lord that you will not cut off my offspring after me, and that you will not destroy my name out of my father's house.' And David swore this to Saul. Then Saul went home, but David and his men went up to the stronghold."

David is reflecting on his promise to protect the house of Saul after he becomes king when he asks a servant in 2 Samuel 9:1, "Is there still anyone left of the house of Saul, that I may show him kindness for Jonathan's sake?" And the servant returns with Mephibosheth, Jonathan's son, a man crippled in his feet. When Saul died, and Jonathan also, his entire family fled, fearing the possibility David would execute them all, as ancient kings did in that day. A nurse carrying Mephibosheth dropped him, and he remained crippled. A crippled person in that day would have suffered greatly. Few would want to take on the burden of caring for someone who could not take care of themselves, but here was Mephibosheth, the son of David's best friend.

David called Mephibosheth to his presence and Mephibosheth fell on his face saying to David in verse 6, "Behold I am your servant." He knew the risk of being called by the "enemy" king. David, probably looking at Mephibosheth and seeing a bit of Jonathan in him, in great emotion and mourning for his friend, says to Mephibosheth in 2 Samuel 9:7, "Do not fear, for I will show you kindness for the sake of your father Jonathan, and I will restore to you all the land of Saul your father, and you shall eat at my table always."

David restored to Mephibosheth what belonged to Jonathan and it is said at the end of the chapter in verse 13, "So Mephibosheth lived in Jerusalem, for he ate always at the king's table. Now he was lame in both feet."

The chapter ends securing Mephibosheth's place in David's kingdom, a rare place of honor at the king's table, and it is not that he was often invited to the king's table as some dignitaries might be, it is that Mephibosheth is invited to the king's table always for every meal. There is a permanent place for him at David's table. He does not need an invitation to David's table just as David does not need an invitation to his own table.

Mephibosheth, broken and incapable of carrying for himself, is so very much like you and me, dear Christ-follower. Like Mephibosheth, you and I have a place at the Lord's table. There is a place for you right now at the Lord's table. It is marked with a permanent placard in bronze or stone, a place secured in the home of God Almighty, a place where you are always welcomed, any meal, any time.

Throughout life, the Lord is taking us through suffering and calm that one day will culminate in the marriage supper of the Lamb in Revelation 19:6-9: "Then I heard what seemed to be the voice of a great multitude, like the roar of many waters and like the sound of mighty peals of thunder, crying out, 'Hallelujah! For the Lord our God the Almighty reigns. Let us rejoice and exult and give him the glory, for the marriage of the Lamb has come, and his Bride has made herself ready; it was granted her to clothe herself with fine linen, bright and pure' – for the fine linen is the righteous deeds of the saints. And the angel said to me, 'Write this: Blessed are those who are invited to the marriage supper of the Lamb.' And he said to me, 'These are the true words of God.'"

As a Christ-follower, this is exactly the place we will be, and these are the exact words we will cry out to the Lord as we are "carried to the table." And here we will be taken care of, our scarred and brokenness passing away and we will have fullness in Christ Jesus, all seated at the table of the Lord!

63

"Untitled Hymn"

"And it is God who establishes us with you in Christ, and has anointed us, and who has also put his seal on us and given us his Spirit in our hearts as a guarantee."

~ 2 Corinthians 1:21-22

"Untitled Hymn" by Chris Rice

In every part of life, we need Jesus, from the storms to the calm, from the exciting to the mundane. We need Jesus in every part. The beauty of "Untitled Hymn" is that the song draws us to every part of life to better declare Jesus' role in each part of our lives. From storms to calms this hymn centers the various joys and troubles of this world onto Christ, who above all can handle the cares and joys of our lives. The song has been a simple, deep, thoughtful, and meaningful part of my life for many years, and I pray it will draw you closer to the Lord, knowing His tender care for each of His beloved children. The longing of my heart and I pray your heart also is Jesus, Jesus, Jesus!

And with each part of life with Christ, you can come to, sing to, fall on, cry to, dance for, and fly to Jesus and at the end of it all to LIVE!

⚓ ⚓ ⚓

63

"Only Jesus"

"For there is one God, and there is one mediator between God and men, the man Christ Jesus."

~ 1 Timothy 2:5

"Only Jesus" by Casting Crowns

———◆———

All of our lives, we have been told to leave a mark, a legacy. We have been told to "make a name the world remembers." But at the end of the day, what does it matter? Does it matter where our name is left? Think about all those people before us who gave tons of money to put their name on a building. How many even notice? This is a morbid question, but have you ever thought of what people would say at your funeral? Will they say how nice you were? Will they say how mean you were? Will they be crying or cheering? What will they say? What legacy will you leave?

Billions of people have passed before us; who were they? What were their stories? What impact did they have? What legacy did they leave? The sad thing about the billions and billions of people that have ever existed and will ever exist is that they are unremembered. And to be honest with you, there will be a day when we will be unremembered. Yes, someone will mourn your passing, but at some point in the future, there will be one person who will be the last person on earth who will remember you.

The beauty of this song is that it reminds us that as Christ-followers, our legacy is not in us, it is in Christ. And the beauty of our passing is that Christ is proclaimed over us. Christ is the only name we should leave behind, "Only Jesus."

All the kingdoms built; all the trophies won

Will crumble into dust when it's said and done

'Cause all that really mattered

Did I live the truth to the ones I love?

Was my life the proof that there is only One

Whose name will last forever?

And I, I don't want to leave a legacy

I don't care if they remember me

Only Jesus

And I, I've only got one life to live

I'll let every second point to Him

Only Jesus

Jesus is the only name

Jesus is the only name

Jesus is the only name to remember

64

"Breathe"

"I have said these things to you, that in me you may have peace. In the world you will have tribulation. But take heart; I have overcome the world."

~ John 16:33

"Breathe" by Jonny Diaz

I have lived in California my entire life, and though I am not a beach bum, the beach is in my soul like any true Californian; although I admit that I do not go as often as I would like. When I go to the beach, I walk onto the beach to find my spot where I can plant myself for a few hours; I stand taking a look around, listening to waves crashing on the shore, and then take a deep breath of that fresh salty air. It is a moment to me where the world is at peace. Life is at peace. Truly at the beach, the world and its problems have no place. Life can be so chaotic that we must relish these moments where we can catch our breath, take in the fresh air, wake up, and move on in life.

One of the beautiful things as a trial ends is taking a deep breath, sighing and opening your eyes to a new future. There is a calm that comes in pausing for a moment, closing your eyes, and taking that deep breath. For those who have seen the end of a trial, this is a moment where we quietly proclaim to our souls, "It's over!" This may be a specific moment or a slow realization. I realized that my cancer crisis was over when doctors started saying, "We no longer need to see you." Those doctors were so instrumental in this part of my life that it was hard to think that I may not see them again. But that is healthy, that is recovery, and that is a sign that life is starting again.

The thing I love about Johnny Diaz's song is that it is a reminder to stop, take a deep breath before the Lord, and rest in what He has done and how he has given you life again and a new perspective.

65

"Save My Life"

"Heal me, O Lord, and I shall be healed; save me, and I shall be saved, for you are my praise."

~ Jeremiah 17:14

"Save My Life" by Sidewalk Prophets

---◆---

This is going to sound weird, but I love my grocery store. Yes, I do! They do not always have what I need or the quantity I need, and when they move things, I can't find anything and freak out. But when Friday afternoon comes around, and I leave work to go to the store, it means I get to buy food and the weekend is here. It also means I get to meet some amazing people who are friendly and enjoyable to be around. I think about the people in your lives that you see regularly, talk to, and have shared stories with. The checker at the grocery store, the pharmacist at the drug store, the server at a restaurant you love, the front desk at your building or workplace, your child's teacher, and the list goes on. Do you know their names? Do you know their story?

These are people we may not give much attention to, or have much concern about; we may even think these are people who are there to serve us, which is a horrible, horrible thought. But these are people in need of Jesus Christ and the salvation He provides, just as you were before you came to Christ. This is not an obligation like, "Okay, God wants me to do this, I do not want to, but whatever, here is the gospel." God's creation is calling out for truth, for hope, for an existence where life all makes sense.

Our storms give us a story, give us part of our testimony to share the gospel with someone. Get to know someone in the doctor's office, at the pharmacy, wherever you may frequent. We have a huge field of people in our lives to start planting the seeds of the gospel, but we have to take the risk of getting out of our comfort zone to engage with an increasingly hostile culture.

I assume you pray for those you love, but do you pray for those you may not love? Do you pray for those you do not really know? Even a mere prayer for someone you do not know is more of God than they may get in a day. Some people we meet will never have a prayer lifted up to the Lord on their behalf. We assume a lot in the church that people care for us and lift us up to the Father, especially during our times of suffering, but for the majority of the world's population, no one is. No one is saying the tiniest of prayers to the Lord for them. And a small, simple prayer is just the base of what we can do for humanity and the neighbors around us. We can share the gospel with them. Jesus is humanity's greatest hope. We hold the solution to the greatest crisis history has ever seen, in men and women never hearing the gospel and being condemned to hell because we did not want to reach out to them, to pray for them. Our job is not to choose who is or is not worthy of the gospel, because at one point you were not worthy, and someone took the time to share the goodness of God's salvation with you. In some ways, by not sharing the gospel, we are sending someone to hell, and who are we to choose who or who not to share the gospel with. Before Christ we are all unworthy.

None of us are worthy, but as Christ-followers, we have been given a great job, a great commission to do. Remember these last words of Jesus. As they were told to His disciples, so they are told to you, commanded by Him. "And Jesus came and said to them, 'All authority in heaven and on earth has been given to me. Go therefore and make disciples of all nations, baptizing them in the name of the Father and of the Son and of the Holy Spirit, teaching them to observe all that I have commanded you. And behold, I am with you always, to the end of the age'" (Matthew 28:18-20).

66

"Where I Belong"

"For none of us lives to himself, and none of us dies to himself. For if we live, we live to the Lord, and if we die, we die to the Lord. So whether we live or whether we die, we are the Lord's. For to this end Christ died and lived again, that he might be Lord both of the dead and of the living."

~ Romans 14:7-9

"Where I Belong" by Switchfoot

The song starts with the lines, "Feeling like a refugee ... this earth is strange to me ... storms on the wasteland ... born into the fight." This is the world you and I were born into, but this is not the world we were made for. This world is foreign to us; we do not belong here, and if you and I really were to consider from birth, we were born into a fight. This is not a world made for God's created ones; it is broken. Here we are, knowing something is not right, but here we build our lives. Deep down inside we know something is terribly wrong in our world.

As Christ-followers, you and I are very aware of what our fight is, why our fight is, and in great joy, we know the fight is over. It is just a matter of time when that ultimate victory of Christ's resurrection is completely fulfilled and finished when He sets all things right in Him. He is patient, and allows this foreign land we live in to continue on that before recreating things, so that many may come to faith in Him.

In our new world in Christ, as new believers, the "weak are made strong ... the righteous right wrongs ... fighting against the tide ... see a generation awaken up inside." We have a long way to go to see our lives, physical and spiritual, restored to the creation God intended, in a world of His creation and full control. Here we are, and here we stand, saved by and living for Christ, in a world we do not belong, but we forge ahead in the life Christ has given us and "live it like a song."

67

"Who You Say I Am"

"Rooted and built up in him and established in the faith, just as you were taught, abounding in thanksgiving."

~ Colossians 2:7

"Who You Say I Am" by Hillsong Worship

In the church, we often talk about how the old us is gone and in Christ, we are new. You are not declared new on your own, but you are declared new because God has declared you new. We will spend our lifetime on earth learning about the new us while fighting the old us in many ways. We know who we were and are learning who we are in Christ.

As the title to the song implies, we are "who you say I am." We are who God says we are, no longer what the world says we are. We are found, we are saved, we are a Child of God. The entire song is about who we were, what Christ has done, and who we are in Christ. The chorus is just glorious, and when we have sung it at church, it is an anthem coming from the depths of our souls,

Who the Son sets free

Oh is free indeed

I'm a child of God

Yes I am

In my Father's house

There's a place for me

I'm a child of God, Yes I am

Whatever your trial was, it is no longer, and this time out of the storm is the time when we can take a deep breath, settle ourselves for a moment, reflect on what God has done, and remember who you are.

I am chosen

Not forsaken

I am who You say I am

You are for me

Not against me

I am who You say I am

68

"Move (Keep Walkin')"

"But we have this treasure in jars of clay, to show that the surpassing power belongs to God and not to us. We are afflicted in every way, but not crushed; perplexed, but not driven to despair; persecuted, but not forsaken; struck down, but not destroyed; always carrying in the body of the death of Jesus, so that the life of Jesus may also be manifested in our bodies. For we who live are always being given over to death for Jesus's sake, so that the life of Jesus also may be manifested in our mortal flesh. So death is at work in us, but life in you."

~ 2 Corinthians 4:7-12

"Move (Keep Walkin')" by TobyMac

———— ♦ ————

TobyMac's song is another one of the songs in this book that truly can help in the storm and the calm, in the bad days and good days. It is a song that fits all parts of life that no matter what the day brings, "Move, keep walkin'." No matter what is happening in life we press on; we keep going despite the days and seasons of our lives.

Another heartbreak day

Feels like you're miles away

Don't even need no shade

When your sun don't shine, shine

Too many passin' dreams

Roll by like limousines

It's hard to keep believin'

When they pass you by and by

I know your heart be broke again

I know your prayers ain't been answered yet

I know you're feeling like you got nothing left

Well, lift your head, it ain't over yet, ain't over yet

Paul brings a more biblical view to our daily plight. He says, "We are afflicted in every way, but not crushed; perplexed, but not driven to despair; persecuted, but not forsaken; struck down, but not destroyed; always carrying in the body of the death of Jesus, so that the life of Jesus may also be manifested in our bodies" (2 Corinthians 4:8-10). Despite what happens in our lives—afflicted, perplexed, persecuted, struck down—Paul reminds us that despite what happens, all these things that we have experienced in this life are nothing compared to God's work in our lives. Despite what happens to us, we are not crushed, not driven to despair, not forsaken, not destroyed. No matter what happens in our lives, we are not taken down or out of the fight because of God's presence in our lives. So Move, Keep Walkin'!

Hold on, hold on

Lord ain't finished yet

Hold on, hold on

He'll get you through this

Hold on, hold on

These are the promises

I will never forget

I will never forget

69

"Because He Lives"

"The thief comes only to steal and kill and destroy. I came that they may have life and have it abundantly."

~ John 10:10

"Because He Lives" by Matt Maher

———◆———

Before you read on, listen to this song. It says so much more than I could say. It is a beautiful song of declaring what you believe about God and how God has worked in our lives. A key line for me, "Because He lives, I can face tomorrow." Because of Christ and what Christ did, we can face anything that life throws at us. Because Christ went to the cross, we have life.

Our trials' reality is that just because we have one trial, major or minor, this does not mean that we will not have another one. There is no "Get out of _____" card in our lives. Some of us will never see the end of suffering in their lives. Some will end a trial only to begin a new trial a short bit later. It would be nice if we had one time of suffering; and that was that, but it is not. However, whatever tomorrow brings, you have life, you have the presence of the Spirit in you to get you through whatever tomorrow brings "because He lives!"

This sinful world has stolen so much from all of us, believer and unbeliever alike. We are not living life as God intended in creation, but the beauty of Christ is that He is life, not just that He gives life, which He does, but He is life. "I'm alive, I'm alive because He lives." One day, we Christ-believers are going to live the life God intended before the dawn of creation, walking with God in the cool of the day, living with God in His house that He built in a room that He personally wrote your name on its door. Christ came from Heaven to earth, to take up the cross, to die on the cross for us, and to defeat death and rise again, so that you and I may face tomorrow. "Because He lives!"

70

"Safe"

"Be strong and courageous. Do not fear or be in dread of them, for it is the Lord your God who goes with you. He will never leave you or forsake you."

~ Deuteronomy 31:6

"Safe" by Phil Wickham

———◆———

When you were a kid, do you remember what you dreamed your future would be like? Who would you be in your 20's? Your 30's? Your 40's? What age would you live to? What career would you pursue? How much of the world would you see before you are 30 or even 40? Who would you marry? How many kids would you have? In your dreams, what did life look like?

I ask those questions, not to bring back those dreams that happened or that did not happen the way you dreamed. Our dreams can give such hope and delight as kids and as we grow and our dreams change or are unfulfilled, it brings us to the point of despair at times. Our trials may have seized some of those dreams. Phil Wickham sings to our dreams and our trials,

To the one whose dreams are falling all apart

And all you're left with is a tired and broken heart

I can tell by your eyes you think you're on your own

But you're not alone

Your trials have taken so much, and it physically and emotionally has taken its toll on you. Still, the realities of the present I pray will create new dreams, new hopes of growing closer to Jesus, becoming more like Jesus.

I leave you with Wickham's chorus:

You will be safe in His arms

You will be safe in His arms

'Cause the hands that hold the world are holding your heart

This is the promise He made

He will be with you always

When everything is falling apart

You will be safe in His arms

And though those dreams of long ago may be gone, dwell on the true reality of being in Christ. "You will be safe in His arms!"

71

"Beautiful"

"And God saw everything that he had made, and behold, it was very good. And there was evening and there was morning, the sixth day."

~ **Genesis 1:31**

"Beautiful" by MercyMe

———◆———

Have you ever contemplated the idea that God chose how tall you would be, the color of your hair, the type of smile you have, the color of your eyes? God took and molded you into who you are and what you look like. Our world condemns itself, as we sometimes condemn ourselves each morning when we get ready for work, for life, even for church. We venture out of the house and see others that, according to the culture, are better looking, or better financed that it seems we will never match up to others. And that is just before we leave the house.

If we look on social media (while it can be a blessing, it is one of the 21st centuries greatest curscs), we see picture-perfect families. We are so good at showing our best sides, even our best-photoshopped sides, but behind those perfect portraits and families, we are not always honest about the issues everyone faces behind closed doors. We make assumptions about others that their lives are perfect while ours are not. But are we looking to this world, even to the Christian culture, for affirmation that we have made it? Or are we looking to God who can only give lasting affirmation in His son, Jesus Christ?

We struggle with life—particularly when others are more beautiful, stronger, richer, talented, and popular -- because we live in a world of sin. When we long to be someone else, to live someone else's life, we have forgotten Genesis 1:26-28a: "Then God said, 'Let us make man in our image, after our likeness. And let them have dominion over the fish of the sea and the birds of the heavens and the livestock and all the earth and over every creeping thing that creeps on the earth.' So God created man in his own image, in the image of God, he created him; male and female he created them.' And God blessed them." We forget God's handiwork in our lives, that God chose you to be as unique as you are, yet sometimes we are not pleased with it.

There is always someone better, and we need to realize there always will be someone better, no matter what stage of life we are in. Even in the nursing home, there will be that old man or woman who can out-Bingo you. Remember this though, in God's eyes, He has a huge smile on His face when he looks at you because He knows you are someone special. God smiles with one look at you, and that is the only smile that should ever matter!

72

"Remind Me Who I Am"

"Do not be conformed to this world, but be transformed by the renewal of your mind, that by testing you may discern what is the will of God, what is good and acceptable and perfect."

~ Romans 12:2

"Remind Me Who I Am" by Jason Gray

———— ♦ ————

Our world is deceptive. It wants us to believe lies to forget the truth. While our trials can be times of clarifications of our relationship with the Lord, our times of calm can often create muddled truths of who we are. We exit the storm with a refreshed perspective, but as we get used to a life without a trial, we drift back into the old life. In 2015 I remember wanting to keep the closeness and intimacy of my walk with the Lord without the distractions of the world and a life outside of the storm. Still, it was a natural transition into life, and the daily distractions we face each and every day returned. Over time the intimacy dissipates. And at all times, we need to continue pursuing the Lord no matter where we are in life.

In this time out of the storm, we will drift back to some of the distractions of life we had before the storm. Yes, we have changed, and as much as we have changed there are years of life outside the storm that is innate within us. Jason Gray wants to help us in praying to the Lord, "Remind Me Who I Am."

Tell me, once again

Who I am to You, who I am to You?

Tell me, lest I forget

Who I am to You, that I belong to You

To You

If there is one thing that has remained stable in our lives and has not changed through the chaos of thousands of years, it is the Bible and its author, God Almighty. And like in the trials of our lives, we must be just as dependent on the Word and the life it brings during the calm as we were during our storm. When we are in the Word, we know exactly who we are. We are His, now and forever!

73

"Live Like That"

"Whoever says he abides in him ought to walk in the same way he walked."

~ 1 John 2:6

"Live Like That" by Sidewalk Prophets

In some ways this is an opposing post to "Only Jesus" by Casting Crowns, but hang in there because it all comes down to Jesus and Jesus alone.

So, here is a totally random and completely self-centered thought for you. What do people say about you, both in front of and behind your back? Might be wise at some point to sit down with a good friend and get the truth of who you really are because who you really are is what people really see. As Christ-followers, the hope should be that when they see us, they see Christ. It is like this, you cannot attend your own funeral, but what if you could, what would people say from the front of the room? What would people mumble from seats in the room? In some ways, it does not matter what people think of us, but in other ways, it does because if we are in Christ, then what people say is a reflection on Him, whether good or bad. I can only pray we do not want to be a bad witness for Christ.

As you consider the legacy you leave, ask yourself and reflect on these questions:

- How are you a representative of Christ and the gospel? What needs to change?

- Was I love when no one else would show up?

- Were you Jesus to the least of these?

- Have you given it all you can?

- Does everything in your life point to Jesus?

- Do you live like your love is true?

- Is there evidence of your faith in your life? If so, what is that evidence?

- When people see you, do they see Jesus?

- How do you bring glory to the King?

74

"There Will be a Day"

"Then I saw heaven opened, and behold, a white horse! The one sitting on it is called Faithful and True and in righteousness he judges and makes war. His eyes are like a flame of fire, and on his head are many diadems, and he has a name written that no one knows but himself. He is clothed in a robe dipped in blood, and the name by which he is called is The Word of God. And the armies of heaven, arrayed in fine linen, white and pure, were following him on white horses. From his mouth comes a sharp sword with which to strike down the nations, and he will rule them with a rod of iron. He will tread the winepress of the fury of the wrath of God the Almighty. On his robe and on his thigh he has a name written, King of kings and Lord of lords."

~ Revelation 19:11-16

"There Will be a Day" by Jeremy Camp

---◆---

The first line of "There Will be a Day" hits so close to home and resonates so deeply in these times between trials and returning to a calm life:

> I try to hold onto this world with everything I have
>
> But I feel the weight of what it brings, and the hurt that tries to grab
>
> The many trials that seem to never end ...

It says so much about our life in this sinful world. We only know this world; this world is home, but home is heavy, and it hurts. We long for a perfect world. As much as we try to create this perfect home, deep down inside we know this world is not perfect, and at the dawn of each day we know it will never be perfect.

But "There Will Be a Day" when we will see "Jesus face to face," and at the moment we transition from this world to Christ's world. We will be made new—no more tears, no more suffering—a world complete, a world renewed. And as you move out of the storm for the moment, I pray you are being renewed. But be renewed knowing that this life is imperfect, and we must continue the fight to live a life completely and absolutely devoted to Christ. This day is coming, but for now, we are here, and we are in Christ. As long as we are in Christ, we can rest in the goodness of Christ's return and a world where it is all His, "a place of no more suffering."

75

"This is Home"

"My people will live in peaceful dwelling places, in secure homes, in undisturbed places for rest."

~ Isaiah 32:18 (NIV)

"This is Home" by Switchfoot

———————◆———————

This song plays a special role in my life. I first fell in love with it when I was in the process of buying my townhome. It was an anthem to have a place that was mine, a place that had my name on it, a place to call my own. It is such an American thing to feel, but it did feel good.

While I loved the song, I quickly realized it was not about home on this earth. Throughout the book, I have mentioned that this world is not for us; it is corrupted; it is drenched in sin. It is all we know, but is it really home? In my mind, when I was buying my home, it was a sense of permanency, but this world isn't permanent; nothing in it is. It is not home.

There are two beauties of "This is Home" that can guide us through our lives in the calm. First, our home is not here. We spend so much time creating, building, furnishing, and making our lives here. The reality of our existence in Christ this side of Heaven is that home is not in a specific place on this earth; with Christ we are home. I remember a sign my mom had when I was a kid that said, "Home is where the heart is," and in Christ, that is true. He is our home, and when we go to Heaven, we will be in His physical presence and His physical home.

The second thing from "This is Home" is the line, "And I won't go back, back to how it was." The beauty of our trials is that we can reflect on who we were and choose to change, choosing not to be who we were and moving on to who Christ wants us to be. The beauty of our sufferings is the refining process that allows us to remove what is unlike Christ from our lives and put on what is Christ, to be more like Him.

As you think about life ahead, dwell on the greatness of Heaven, being in the presence of Jesus. Consider how life needs to change, how you need to change. This post-trial calm gives us a "brand new mindset" and "I can finally see the sunset." What a glorious thing for us to see the last sunset on earth and our first sunrise with Christ, a sunrise at home ... on into eternity.

76

"Whatever You're Doing"

"Now may the God of peace who brought again from the dead our Lord Jesus, the great shepherd of the sheep, but the blood of the eternal covenant, equip you with everything good that you may do his will, working in us that which is pleasing in his sight, through Jesus Christ, to whom be glory forever and ever. Amen."

~ Hebrews 13:20-21

"Whatever You're Doing (Something Heavenly)" by Sanctus Real

As you read the following opening lines to the song, think back to your trial, however hard or easy that may be.

It's time for healing, time to move on

It's time to fix what's been broken too long

Time to make right what has been wrong

It's time to find my way to where I belong

There's a wave that's crashing over me

And all I can do is surrender

You are now in a place no longer in the trial, but maybe not ready to move on. Maybe you're not exactly or entirely healed, but you know it is time. It could take a lifetime to process what you have just gone through, whether it was in your recent or distant past. I am here going on five years clear of cancer, yet still trying to make sense of all that happened. The song's first line says it all: "It's time for healing, time to move on." God doesn't want us to stay static in life, no matter how much we want life to stay the same. Life is change. We were never meant to stay the same; we were meant to grow in who we are. And in this time of calm, we need time to take what we have learned and use it for the Lord and His kingdom.

In *Anchored in the Storm*, I mentioned a text my pastor sent me while I went through cancer. He said, "Continue to let the waves of fear crash over you and meet God on the other side." The fear of being in the stormy sea is gone, but the waves are going to continue coming, as they always do on the beach, even in these days of restoration. Those waves of healing, just as those waves of suffering, still have to go over God to get to you. Those gracious hands of God have to work, just as much as they did during our trials, in our healing, in our recovery. God has a mighty work to do throughout our entire lives, but more poignantly in these bright light and gloomy dark days. As we surrendered our lives to Him in our trial, this is a time to revive, to recover, to learn more, to grow more to reflect and to refine. The refining process continues; it's never finished this side of Heaven.

The chorus sounds very much like our trials:

Whatever You're doing inside of me

It feels like chaos but I believe

You're up to something bigger than me

Larger than life, something Heavenly

This time of healing will hurt. Like a wound closing up, it takes time. For some wounds, there will be scars. And amongst the chaos and the thoughts rushing through your mind, consider the Lord. He was present in your storm, and He is present in your calm. He is doing something that at this moment you may not understand. But God knows what He is doing. That should be the only thing that matters during this time. God is doing a great work in your life, and as Sanctus Real sings to God, "You're up to something bigger than me ... Larger than life, something Heavenly." God is working on something bigger than each of our lives, but He is using us in all parts of life for "something Heavenly."

It's time to face up, clean this old house

Time to breathe in and let everything out

77

"Nobody, Everybody, Somebody"

"Jesus said to [Thomas], 'I am the way, and the truth, and the life. No one comes to the Father except through me. If you had known me, you would have known my Father also. From now on you do know him and have seen him."

~ John 14:6-7

"Nobody"* by Casting Crowns

———— ♦ ————

One of the sad states of our present day, among many, is that each of us thinks we are somebody. We think our looks, our friends, our zip code, and our "likes" on social media, all make us significant. Since Adam and Eve, every person in every part of the world and in every time period, has thought that they are significant. The sad reality of this deception is that at this moment there are almost 8 billion "significant" and "special" people on this earth, yet each one of us is the most significant, the most special. I have to chuckle because no matter what, there will always be someone who enters a room thinking they are "all that".

Reality can be a sobering, humbling, maybe humiliating, precious gift to us. It is the truth of who we are over the truth of who God is. Yes, in some ways, we are significant in this world, but as humans, not always as individuals. Above it all, God is SIGNIFICANT! His presence, His character, His actions, everything that God is, has far more impact and influence than any single person ever. God is it; He is what makes us significant.

The reality we need to hear in all of us is that we are "nobody." In the scheme of human history, in the expanse of the universe, in the presence of God Almighty, you and I are absolutely "nobody." But that's where the beauty of God's hand in His creation comes in. Because we are "nobody," we can express the greatness of this "somebody" working throughout history in the universe. He is God Almighty and as "nobody's" we are given so much to tell this world about our great "SOMEBODY."

Your story is the story of "somebody" working such extraordinary works in the life of a "nobody," and I pray you will take the story of the work of God in your life and go out and tell "everybody" about His work:

'Cause I'm just a nobody trying to tell everybody

All about Somebody who saved my soul

Ever since You rescued me, You gave my heart a song to sing

I'm living for the world to see nobody but Jesus

I'm living for the world to see nobody but Jesus

*The reality of the "nobodies" of this song is that we mean the absolute world to God, the one "somebody." God says of humanity in Genesis 1:28, "And God blessed them." and later in verse 31, "And God saw everything that he had made and behold, it was very good." God did not say we were just good, but He specifically said, "very good." In light of the almost 8 billion of us on this earth, you and I are truly a "nobody," but you and I serve the greatest "somebody" ever.

78

"Burn the Ships"

"Remember not the former things, nor consider the things of old. Behold, I am doing a new thing, now it springs forth, do you not perceive it? I will make a way in the wilderness and rivers in the desert."

~ Isaiah 43:18-19

"Burn the Ships" by for KING & COUNTRY

When our trials and sufferings are nearing the end or are over, the Lord gives us many opportunities to change our lives. We have learned a lot, and in some ways, lost a lot. This time out of the storm is an opportunity to pick up the pieces of some of our lives, but in another way is an even larger opportunity to move on, to let go, and to burn the ships.

What does it mean to burn the ships? "Burn the ships" is a phrase seemingly from the Spanish conquest of the New World. Arriving in the New World in 1519, Hernan Cortes was on a mission to conquer Mexico for Spain. His 600 men were tired and eager to return to the lives they left back in Spain. Cortes, having just landed in Mexico, faced the possibility of not fulfilling his mission because the men longed for what had been. In what is a bold move, he had the ships they travelled on burned. The men had no choice but to take a breath, pick up what was left, and move on towards the Spanish conquest of Mexico, whether good or bad.

You and I are not out to conquer lands, but we do look back at what we had with longing, and in many ways, we look at what we have lost in our suffering as a loss. In our suffering, God has burned our ships to the past and is exhorting us to pick up where we stand and move on, up the path He has for us in the future.

Looking at our burning ship from the beach, we"

Step into a new day

We can rise up from the dust and walk away

We can dance upon the heartache, yeah

So light a match, leave the past, burn the ships

And don't you look back

This time out of the storm is a significant opportunity for us to take account of what is important in our lives and move ahead with a God who will send you on spectacular paths you have never imagined.

So take that deep breath of air in this new life you have. Take a look at those burning ships, embrace the hand of God, and walk on into what is going to be an epic adventure with Him!

⚓ ⚓ ⚓

79

Faith on Fire - Part One

"O Nebuchadnezzar, we have no need to answer you in this matter. If this be so, our God whom we serve is able to deliver us from the burning fiery furnace, and he will deliver us out of your hand, O king. But if not, be it known to you, O king, that we will not serve your gods or worship the golden image that you have set up."

~ Daniel 3:16b-18

———◆———

By the 6th century B.C., the great kings of Israel were gone, the kingdom itself had split up, and the Jewish people were forced from their promised land to Babylon. They had been in exile for some years when the book of Daniel was written. Four people stand out because of their faith.

Daniel, of course, is one, and then the trio of Shadrach, Meshach, and Abednego. All four served the Babylonian king, Nebuchadnezzar, most likely as eunuchs. Because of the great wisdom, strength, and boldness the Lord had given them a place in a hostile kingdom they served the Lord by serving Nebuchadnezzar. Yet the four made incredible decisions to risk it all for the sake of the Lord.

In Daniel 3, we learn that the king created a huge golden statue. All the people of Babylon were to bow and worship the image when a plethora of instruments rang out. Nebuchadnezzar was king, a god to the Babylonians and their captured masses. If anyone dared not to bow down in worship to the statue when the music played, they were executed. Nebuchadnezzar had prepared a great oven to burn any dissident alive.

Shadrach, Meshach, and Abednego were faithful only to one God, not the god of Nebuchadnezzar, but the God of Abraham, Isaac, and Jacob. There was God and no other, and only to Him would they bow and give their allegiance. This proves to be a problem for Shadrach, Meshach, and Abednego. When the music played and the masses bowed, there stood the three in defiance. They were not going to bow to the king, and they surely were not going to bow to the golden image.

The king seeing their disobedience, calls them out, declaring to the crowd, "But if you do not worship, you shall immediately be cast into a burning fiery furnace. And who is the god who will deliver you out of my hands?" Shadrach, Meshach, and Abednego knew they faced certain death, and Nebuchadnezzar mocked the God they were willing to give their life for. He is challenging them, "Who is this god? I am the only one that can deliver you from the fire." He was declaring himself to be a god who needed to be worshipped and bowed down to.

In great boldness, Shadrach, Meshach, and Abednego respond, "O Nebuchadnezzar, we have no need to answer you in this matter. If this be so, our God whom we serve is able to deliver us from the burning fiery furnace, and he will deliver us out of your hand, O king. But if not, be it known to you, O king, that we will not serve your gods or worship the golden image that you have set up." (Daniel 3:16b-18). Can you imagine saying that before a great world leader? "Yeah, that's nice, but we're not going to do that." But here they stood, ready to take the consequence. And Nebuchadnezzar was willing to give them.

In anger and rage, he ordered the fires of the furnace seven times hotter than normal. Once the heat was on, the three men were taken by soldiers directly to the furnace. "Because the king's order was urgent and the furnace overheated, the flame of the fire killed those men who took up Shadrach, Meshach, and Abednego" (Daniel 3:22). Shadrach, Meshach, and Abednego fell into the fire. The crowd reacted with a gasp. They had just seen the soldiers burned up by the fire, the three men had fallen into the fire, and as they all looked, they saw not three men, but four in the midst of the fire. Astonished, Nebuchadnezzar tells his advisors, "But I see four men, unbound, walking in the midst of the fire, and they are not hurt; and the appearance of the fourth is like a son of the gods" (Daniel 3:25).

Nebuchadnezzar called out to the three declaring them to be "servants of the Most High God." They came out intact, without a burn, or stench, as if they had not even been in the fire. In a complete turnaround from the start of the chapter and the creation of the golden image, the king worshipped God; "Blessed be the God of Shadrach, Meshach, and Abednego, who has sent his angel and delivered his servants, who trusted in him, and set aside the king's command, and yielded up their bodies rather than serve and worship any god except their own God" (Daniel 3:28). Shadrach, Meshach, and Abednego are given promotions in the service of Nebuchadnezzar, and God is worshipped in Babylon.

Your testimony and faith are on the line. Some people will look at God's work in your life and casually and curtly say, "That's nice." and change the subject. Some people will be antagonistic towards you because of your faith and excitement about your experience with the Lord. And there will be others who will persecute you because of your faith, because of your story, either to your face or behind your back. You may be insulted, but even more than that is that God is insulted. His name is being put on the line, and as you are in Him, so you are putting yourself out there. But your witness, your declaration is to be just like Shadrach, Meshach, and Abednego. We say "We serve Christ and Christ alone and we're not going to back down from that, even to the point of death." Shadrach, Meshach, and Abednego did not know what would happen as they walked toward certain death. They thought they were going to die. As they walked through the fires, their faith was emboldened, lit up because right with them was Jesus Himself, an epiphany. And when you walk into those fires in this life, you may not make it without getting singed or burned. However because of the Lord, we will walk out of the furnace eager to continue, knowing we serve a God who is going to defend us, who is going to show up exactly when He has planned and purposed. We may not get a promotion because of our faith; we may see death as many martyrs have over the centuries. Still, God will show up; He will be with us in every moment because God is a faithful God, not a golden image. He is a God who is alive and eager for His name to be proclaimed before a disbelieving world.

"If this be so, our God whom we serve is able to deliver us from the burning fiery furnace, and he will deliver us out of your hand, O king" (Daniel 3:17).

80

Faith on Fire - Part Two

"For he is the living God, enduring forever, his kingdom shall never be destroyed, and his dominion shall be to the end. He delivers and rescues; he works signs and wonders in heaven and on earth, he who has saved Daniel from the power of the lions."

~ Daniel 6:26b-27

———◆———

By the time Daniel gets his time in the "fiery furnace," his friends Shadrach, Meshach, and Abednego are off the scene, and Nebuchadnezzar and the Babylonian empire had fallen to the Persians. Years, maybe decades have passed between Daniel 3 and 6. Darius, king of the Medes and Persians is now ruling, and Daniel holds a place of great power in the nation. In Daniel 6:3 it says, "Daniel became distinguished above all the other high officials and satraps, because an excellent spirit was in him. And the king planned to set him over the whole kingdom."

Before Darius, Daniel's position before the nation was not entirely accepted by others, especially as a Jewish exile. Many had seen Daniel's faith in God and the talents given to him through the Lord and were intensely jealous of his position. Those jealous of Daniel schemed behind the scenes to find ways to entrap him as a way to take him out of power. A plan was developed and presented to Darius. They said, "O, King Darius, live forever! All the high officials of the kingdom, the high officials and the satraps, the counselors, and the governors are agreed that the king should establish an ordinance and enforce an injunction, that whoever makes petition to any god or man for thirty days, except to you, O king, shall be cast into the den of lions" (Daniel 6:6b-7). Another part of the injunction Darius agreed to was that the law could not be changed. Knowing the law and that it could not be revoked, Darius signed it. The trap was set. Everyone in the kingdom was to worship only Darius for 30 days. If they did not, they were sent to a den of lions, and you can imagine what torment would be there before an eventual death.

In his powerful position, Daniel, knew exactly what happened, the exact words of the law, and what this meant for him as a man faithful to God. He was not a boisterous man who was willing to challenge the system. He had seen Shadrach, Meshach, and Abednego and their test of faith, and here was his. He is going to take a bold move. "When Daniel knew that the document had been signed, he went to his house where he had windows in his upper chamber open toward Jerusalem. He got down on his knees three times a day and prayed and gave thanks before God, as he had done previously" (Daniel 6:10). Daniel decided he was not going to change. He knew what was on the line and was willing to pay the price for worshipping the Lord of Abraham, Isaac, and Jacob and not Darius as a god. He knew the consequences of his actions against Darius; everything was on the line.

Darius was told by those seeking Daniel's demise and "was much distressed and set his mind to deliver Daniel. And he labored till the sun went down to rescue him." Daniel was a favorite of Darius, a man well respected by the king. No matter how hard Darius tried, the law was the law, and he was reminded there was nothing he could do. He had to send Daniel to the den of lions or lose all his power and standing as king. His hands were tied, and Daniel had to be sent down to the lions. Grudgingly, Darius had Daniel brought to the den, put in with the lions, and he even put his royal seal on the stone covering the den to ensure his orders were fulfilled.

Darius knew Daniel. He knew that Daniel was not going to worship him. He even declares as Daniel was put down into the den, "May your God, whom you serve continually, deliver you!" (Daniel 6:16).

Darius was tormented through the night with anxiety on whether Daniel was going to survive. He knew Daniel as a faithful man and commended Daniel and Daniel's God before, but Darius was not a faithful man, not a follower of God. He could not eat or sleep, and the pleasures of life were not enjoyed by him because of what he did to Daniel.

At dawn, as the sun was breaking the night, Darius went to the den of lions, eager to release Daniel, if Daniel had survived. The stone is removed, and Darius peeked in to see the state of Daniel. He yelled into the cave, "O Daniel, servant of the living God, has your God, whom you serve continually, been able to deliver you from the lions?" (Daniel 6:20b). Darius knew of Daniel's faithfulness to the Lord and the Lord's faithfulness to Daniel. Daniel exclaims to the king, "O king, live forever! My God sent his angel and shut the lions' mouths, and they have not harmed me because I was found blameless before him; and also, before you, O king, I have done no harm" (Daniel 6: 21b-22).

Daniel had survived not because of Daniel, but because of God. It was always God and Daniel trusted God for his great position in the kingdom and in the lions' den. Daniel was not out to go after Darius, whom he gladly served. His priority above Darius was to serve the Lord in whatever situation was before him.

For both Daniel and Shadrach, Meshach, and Abednego, their faith was on the line. They stayed loyal to their God and disloyal to the government. The government had asked them to do what they could not; to betray the Lord and worship a human king. The consequences for all were clearly declared, and rather than betray God, were willing to take on death for worshipping the Lord. Their faith was no different than yours or mine. No doubt they questioned these things, maybe even questioned God. But like them, and like you, God showed Himself faithful. Even in death, God was still faithful. Daniel, Shadrach, Meshach, and Abednego had all known who they were going to serve; it was not a man or any leader, or anything of this world. It was God, the God who had promised Abraham descendants as numerous as the sands on the beach, a promised land, a covenant with the people. They knew who they served, and in the prosperity of their positions in Babylon and

Persia, as well as in the face of execution, their faith did not waver. They served God when it was good, and when it was bad, in the calm and in the storm. The four men were witnesses to the character, nature, and work of the Lord.

Their testimonies lay not in the heroic actions they undertook for the Lord, but in their relationship with the Lord. They believed that whatever was going to happen, God was going to act. It was not their actions that made a difference; it was God's actions. In their lives, they knew that whatever they faced, the plenty in the kingdoms they served in, the position and power they held, the fiery furnace to the lions' dens, their testimony was the work of God in their lives. Similarly your testimony is not distinctly your situation, but how God is working in your life. Ultimately, Daniel, Shadrach, Meshach, and Abednego are regular people like you and I are. Like us, they want to see God proclaimed above every false god, above every name, above everything this world says and does that God may receive the glory.

Postscript

As a note for Daniel in the lions' den, Darius was greatly pleased that Daniel had survived and in the majesty and power of Daniel's God. In response to Daniel's living through the lions' den, Darius had those who targeted Daniel put into the cavern with the lions, and not just the men, but their wives and children also. They didn't even make it to the bottom of the bit before the lions tore them all to pieces, a gruesome end no doubt.

Darius commends Daniel to the kingdom and exalts God in his kingdom saying, "I make a decree, that in all my royal dominion people are to tremble and fear the God of Daniel, for he is the living God, enduring forever, his kingdom shall never be destroyed, and his dominion shall be to the end. He delivers and rescues; he works signs and wonders in heaven and on earth, he who has saved Daniel from the power of the lions." (Daniel 6:26-27).

81

Speak What You Know

"For we cannot but speak of what we have seen and heard."

~ Acts 4:20

If you had the attention of a crowd with all eyes on you, eager to hear your words, curious as to your presence, what would you say? They are sitting on the edge of their seats and waiting for words you need to say in this memorable moment. What words would you bring to the crowd?

Jesus' disciples, John and Peter, were in this exact situation in Acts 4 as they spoke to the Temple crowds. The crowd before them knew they were close friends of Jesus. They undoubtedly heard about Peter's betrayal of Jesus and of John's faithful presence at Jesus' crucifixion and his personal care of Jesus' mother. These are men of standing and controversy in a shaken Jerusalem. Jesus was gone, yet His followers were all over the place, having returned after the chaos and pain of Jesus' crucifixion. They were changed and challenged, stronger than ever in their faith.

Here John and Peter choose to engage people on the Temple grounds itself, crowds abundant, curiosity even more abundant, including the ever-present critical Jewish religious leaders, the

Pharisees and Sadducees. While the Jewish religious leaders were always questioning Jesus, they are now questioning His disciples, their miracles, and their words. The religious leaders did not appreciate the words of truth spoken to the crowds, that Jesus had fulfilled the Old Testament prophecies, died, and had risen from the dead. Even the religious leaders were aware of this truth. Still, the truth did not come to them. The Messiah they wanted was not the Messiah they got, a sacrificial savior instead of a political savior to challenge the Romans. They could not control the truth of Jesus as Christ—Messiah—so instead of stopping the truth, they stopped those who were speaking the truth; Peter and John were arrested under the direction of the Temple's religious leaders (Acts 4:1-3). The focus of our discussion at the moment are the words preached before the Jewish religious council. Because of this one day, Peter and John's words, 5,000 people came to believe in Jesus Christ as their Lord and Savior.

One day they are preaching the Word; the next they are before the Jewish religious leaders in handcuffs for preaching the Word. I find it fascinating that the Romans did not arrest them; it was the Jewish leaders. So here they are, standing before the same people that executed the King of Kings. The religious leaders under Annas, the high priest, and Caiaphas asked them, "By what power or what name did you do this?" (Acts 4:7b).

The priests are referring to the day before and the incidents in the Temple and the man healed by Peter "in the name of Jesus Christ of Nazareth." Continuing on, Peter argues that this good deed of healing this crippled man, "by the same Jesus Christ of Nazareth whom you crucified whom God raised from the dead— by him this man is standing before you well."

Peter's essentially saying the group knows the power and the person that healed the man; it was the same power that raised Jesus, the healing by God at work. This man that was crippled, who was most likely a regular figure on the Temple grounds, stands before the group, walking, talking, testifying to the work of Christ in his life. Just as Jesus' resurrection, this miracle was performed before the religious leaders. In what is a bold move for Peter, he says to the crowd in the room, "And there is salvation in no one else, for there is no other name under heaven given among men by which we must be saved." The religious leaders were not really after the man who was healed, they were after Jesus and those who followed Him, including the disciples. The council was literally speechless at Peter's bold testimony. There was nothing they could say to oppose what clearly was before them.

The issue really was not the man healed; it was the words declared by Peter and John in the streets of Jerusalem, in the Temple, and now before the council. Jesus was not the Messiah they wanted, and they wanted to stop Jesus' followers from declaring what they had seen, experienced, and heard about the saving power of Jesus' name. They didn't preach an earthly salvation, but an eternal one of reconciliation between God and man. These words of Jesus Christ were, and still are, divisive. Jesus is Lord, and whether spoken from man or creation, they will be spoken of God and salvation in no other than Jesus Christ Himself.

The religious leaders challenge Peter and John to stop preaching the gospel. They did not want the hope and freedom of Christ spread amongst the people. They wanted to stop the spread of salvation, partly because salvation was not of them. Peter and John are well aware of the connection between the religious leaders and the Roman Empire. They are also aware of the power both leaders have over anyone that causes disturbances in the volatile region.

Peter and John stand before the powerful leaders and in what has to be one of the boldest moves in history, declares, "Whether it is right in the sight of God to listen to you rather than to God you must judge ..." (Acts 4:19). Peter and John knew who their ultimate audience was; it was not the religious leaders, it was God Himself. It was God alone who ultimately mattered, not the Jewish religious leaders or the Roman authorities. Continuing on, they declare, "for we cannot but speak of what we have seen and heard" (Acts 4:20). They had been with Jesus for three years. During that time, they saw His death, His resurrection, His work among the people, and His work of salvation among the motley crew of the disciples. Of all people ever in history, they were most knowledgeable of God. They knew Jesus, and the only thing they could do is speak of what they had witnessed. Peter and John had no control over how the religious leaders interpreted their words. Essentially, Peter and John are saying to the council; they can only speak truth and nothing else.

Like Peter and John, you have seen God work in your life. You have seen God work in your salvation. You have spent time praying with God about your life and your circumstances, about other's lives and their circumstances. Hopefully, when you were in the storm, you reached out to God as the only One who can entirely manage your circumstances. We see bits and pieces of God's work in our lives, and only when we enter eternity with Him will we see the entire picture of His work. For now, we have enough of God's handiwork in our lives to speak. I pray that you will see that through your storm you have learned that you now have a strong, vast, and important story to tell, the story of God's work in your life. And if you are someone who is saved but has few trials, you have seen God's grace in your salvation. If our salvation is all we have to tell of God's work in our lives, than that is the greatest story we could ever tell.

I pray for you that wherever you take the opportunity to share the gospel before men or councils, that we will declare like Peter and John before a curious crowd, "for we cannot but speak of what we have seen and heard."

82

Over Happiness

"For the kingdom of God is not a matter of eating and drinking but of righteousness and peace and joy in the Holy Spirit."

~ **Romans 14:17**

I n the United States, our lives from the moment we are born is all about happiness. Even our Declaration of Independence exclaims, "We hold these truths to be self-evident, that all men are created equal, that they are endowed by their Creator with certain unalienable Rights, that among these are Life, Liberty, and the pursuit of Happiness." Since we were born, happiness is a part of our American DNA. It is who we are, and since birth we have been told, maybe not in words, that we are to pursue happiness. Happiness is the priority of our lives, and if you look back on your life, you would see that you have done things because you wanted to be happy, both in righteousness and in sinfulness. For our world, happiness is "a matter of eating and drinking," doing what makes us happy. If the Declaration of Independence says to pursue happiness, we are just fulfilling the American dream when we do pursue it.

But is life just about each of us being happy? So many of us choose and pursue it as a life motto. As we can see from our declining culture, moving from happy moment to happy moment has not made any of us better people. If we look throughout the Bible, happiness is not a word that is used regularly. We see it only ten times in the English Standard Version, which is the version I have used for this book and *Anchored in the Storm*. There are thousands of words in the Bible and ten times is not a lot.

A friend of mine said this years ago when I was in a young adult Bible study, and it has stayed with me ever since, "We must whisper what God whispers and shout what God shouts." Since happiness is not a priority for the Lord, it should not be a priority of ours. God does not want us to pursue temporary things. Happiness is a momentary feeling, and God is not about momentary things; He is about things that will last, that are steady, that are more permanent. Happiness is a part of our world and a part of who we are. But what is more lasting and stable than happiness? The word is … joy!

Joy is sometimes used interchangeably with happiness as in Job 20:4-5 when Job says, "Do you not know this from of old, since man was placed on earth, that the exulting of the wicked is short, and the joy of the godless but for a moment?" While happiness is a matter of emotions, joy is a matter of being, not a matter of circumstances, but a matter of existence. Joy is a position in Christ Jesus as a beloved child. Joy is of the heavens; happiness is of the world.

John MacArthur, in his sermon "Fundamental Christian Attitudes: Joy," says so eloquently that joy "is the experience of well-being—it is the experience of well-being that springs from the deep-down confidence that God is in perfect control of everything, for my good and His glory."

John Piper, in his talk, "How to Define Joy" affirms and expands on MacArthur's definition: "Christian joy is a good feeling in the soul, produced by the Holy Spirit, as He causes us to see the beauty of Christ in the word and in the world." We could say that joy goes to the depths of our existence, not from circumstances, but from the Lord and His Word, a trust that our lives are under the complete control of His hands. Knowing that joy is of God and from God makes the absolute difference in joy versus happiness.

I want to be clear about something. God is not looking to take away all things that make us happy. He does not want us to be a people without pleasure. He also doesn't want us to take that fun from others. Our God has a huge smile on His face when He thinks of you and your walk with Him. But the beauty of God and His choice of joy is first; joy comes from Him, and anything that God gives is good. Happiness does not always come from Him. There are plenty of times when we are in sin that we are perfectly happy. Second, God wants to give us something more than a momentary feeling. Happiness is here for a moment and gone in the blink of an eye. Joy is ours eternal in Christ, a fruit of the Spirit as Paul writes in Galatians 5:22-23; "But the fruit of the Spirit is love, joy, peace, patience, kindness, goodness, faithfulness, gentleness, self-control; against such things there is no law." Happiness is not listed among the signs of the Spirit's presence in our lives.

Relish the presence of the Spirit in your life and in your walk. Pray for better understanding of joy in your life, and instead of pursuing things for failing happiness, pray for a life of joy!

83

Lost and Faith

*"But Ruth said, 'Do not urge me to leave you or to return from fol-
lowing you. For where you go, I will go, and where you lodge, I will
lodge. Your people shall by me people, and your God my God."*

~ Ruth 1:16

---◆---

uth is an odd figure in the Bible. She is not Jewish; she is
not from Judea; she does not believe in God. She is truly
an outlier in all of biblical history. Her entire story in the
book of her name is worth a read. It is short, but God
is working incredibly in this young woman's life. While her story
and connection to the ancestral line of Jesus are paramount in the
biblical narrative, her faith in the face of losing everything takes
her to a place where she gained everything.

Here is a short summary of a short book: Ruth's mother-in-law,
Naomi, and her family left Judah to survive a famine, retreating to
Moab for refuge. Naomi's two sons marry Moabite women, one of
them being Ruth. We do not know the timing, but Naomi's husband and her two sons later died, leaving Naomi, Ruth, and Orpah,
her other daughter-in-law, all widowed. This is a horrendous event,
to say the least, particularly in a time when being a widowed woman without sons or extended family, meant utter poverty.

They have nothing in Moab, no hope, no family, no future. Naomi, despite her barren future as the matriarch of the desperate trio,

knows the Lord's work. She knows God can work through these tragedies. She is not going to have any grand restoration, and at this moment, neither is Ruth. Ruth has spent her hardest days with Naomi, one death after another. Though a very trying experience, Naomi has a faith that stands out to Ruth, a faith in a God unknown in Moab, but if there is this God who can create in Naomi a glimmer of hope, even a hope back in Judah, Ruth wanted it.

She says to Naomi, "Do not urge me to leave you or to return from following you. For where you go, I will go, and where you lodge, I will lodge. Your people shall by me people, and your God my God" (Ruth 1:16). Naomi and Ruth bid farewell to Moab (and Orpah, who stays behind) to return to Judah, knowing nothing of what will happen to them when they return. They return to the area Naomi left so many years ago. Even so, they don't really know anyone around. Naomi remembers a somewhat distant relative, Boaz, who is a kinsmen redeemer of the family. Naomi knows God is at work, through a course of events and prodding by Naomi, the Lord brings Boaz and Ruth together, both of whom are named in the lineage of Christ.

In Moab, Ruth faced an uncertain and likely forgotten future. However, she trusted not in Naomi, but in God, and will be remembered for millennia because of her faith. Her story continues long throughout history.

Your testimony of life and faith in Jesus displayed before a longing world will bring people to Christ. If Naomi and her family had not left Judah, her son would never have married Ruth, and Ruth would never have returned to Judah; she would never have met Boaz or married Boaz, and would not be named among the lineage of Jesus Christ Himself. Naomi would never have anticipated that her loss and trust in God would have the ending it did. She proved herself faithful in the Lord's plan. It was not a perfect faith, and it is a guarantee she had doubts, as you and I do, but she knows God, and any doubts are quickly diminished in the Lord's providence.

Once Ruth gets married, we know very little of what happens to Naomi. Most likely, Ruth and Boaz took her in and cared for her, but that is no guarantee. However, we do have a bit of insight in Naomi's whereabouts. At the end of Ruth, we find a great answer to Naomi's faith and the Lord's work in their lives: "Then the women said to Naomi, 'Blessed be the Lord, who has not left you this day without a redeemer, and may his name be renowned in Israel! He shall be to you a restorer of life and a nourisher of your old age, for your daughter-in-law who loves you, who is more to you than seven sons, has given birth to him" (Ruth 4:14). The last lines of the book of Ruth in verse 16 it says, "Obed fathered Jesse, and Jesse fathered David." David is the king of Israel, and years later, will come Jesus Christ, king of heaven and earth, God Almighty.

Naomi's faith led to Ruth's faith, which led to her and Boaz's marriage, which led to the birth of Ruth's great-grandson David, king of Israel. Faith in the storm and faith in the calm leads to faith in the lives of the future. That faith impacts those who watch from up close and to those who observe from a distance. Your faith will impact someone else, and though Naomi was not alive to see David or to see Christ in His time, she trusted that God was going to work beyond her understanding. She just needed to be faithful to the Lord's provision and purpose for her. Naomi's seemingly small choices of faith played a part in the Lord's plans and such a large role in redemptive history, and even in your own redemption.

Go forth in faith in Christ, not knowing what He is going to do, but trusting that God will do something incredible, even if it is something you will never know of this side of Heaven. We never know what God can do with even the smallest steps of faith.

84

What They Say

"These all died in faith, not having received the things promised, but having seen them and greeted them from afar and having acknowledged that they were strangers and exiles on the earth."

~ Hebrews 11:13

———— ◆ ————

"Others suffered mocking and flogging, and even chains and imprisonment. They were stoned, they were sawn in two, they were killed with the sword. They went about in skins of sheep and goats, destitute, afflicted, mistreated—of whom the world was not worthy—wandering about in deserts and mountains, and in dens and caves of the earth" (Hebrews 11:36-39).

You may or may not know the book of the Bible from which this passage comes from, but do you know what this passage is saying? Who are these people? Why are they allowing this to happen? This seems to be a very dark passage in the New Testament. In some ways, it appears that these victims do not react or respond to their murderers, but why?

The author of Hebrews has given us an incredible chapter of seeing testimonies of many throughout the Bible who put their full faith in Jesus Christ. So many were targeted, harassed, and executed for their faith. The people above were those Christ-followers that this side of heaven remain nameless and aside from their general trials and torments, story-less. The author of Hebrews understands there are too many pages to write to tell of each personal story. Remember how John writes about Jesus in John 21:25: "Now there are also many other things that Jesus did. Were every one of them to be written, I suppose that the world itself could not contain the books that would be written." If there are not enough books to contain all that Jesus did while present on this earth, how many more books that could there be that contain the stories of those who have lived for Him? His work in this world is limitless!

In the passage, the men and women were willing to endure such abhorrent living conditions and deaths as followers of Jesus Christ. For Him, they were willing to forgo a life on this earth like that of their unbelieving peers. Yet, here they are written about in Hebrews 11, a passage we call the Hall of Faith.

Why did these believers throughout time so willingly and gladly stand up for Christ, knowing that they would receive such horrific physical endings? Would you willingly walk into such situations knowing this would be your physical end? These are sobering questions to answer in a world growing more and more critical of those of faith in Christ.

The author of Hebrews tells us why and what brought these people to literally put everything on the line for Christ. He writes in verses 39-40, "And all these, though commended through their faith, did not receive what was promised, since God had provided something better for us, that apart from us they should be made perfect." They knew this world was not their own; it was not their home. They knew God had promised the best life, but not the best life now; it was the best life to come, in the presence of God Almighty in a world completely under His control, created as He intended for those who believe. These mere moments of great suffering were exactly that for them, mere moments. And in these moments, their names are forgotten, but their stories continue as men and women who knew Christ and were willing to do absolutely anything for Him.

These words of their sufferings are left behind and their faith continues. These men and women are commended in the Bible for their faith and trust in Jesus Christ. Their stories remain. Neither you nor I will ever be in the Bible; our stories will disappear within a generation of our passing, maybe two generations, but they will disappear. What will they say about how we suffered and lived? What few words, like those in Hebrews 11, will be used to describe the extremes put upon us for our Lord? What will our lives say, not about us, but about Christ?

This passage is one of the most beautiful writings of this group, and really of all Christ-followers: "Of whom the world is not worthy" (verse 38). The story of Christ is still told 2,000 years later. The story of those who follow Him continue on, and all are not worthy of this world. If you were to be placed in the Hall of Faith in Heaven, what would be written?

85

In All Ways Straight Paths

"Trust in the Lord with all your heart, and do not lean on your own understanding. In all your ways acknowledge him, and he will make straight your paths. Be not wise in your own eyes; fear the Lord, and turn away from evil. It will be healing to your flesh and refreshment to your bones."

~ **Proverbs 3:5-8**

———— ♦ ————

A hope I have in writing these two *Anchored* books is for you to know the Lord more. It is not about what I write, but it is about drawing you closer to Him in a more personal and intimate relationship, that you will spend time in His Word, in prayer, talking with Him, allowing Him to work in your life and partnering with Him in bringing the light of the gospel to a world steeped in utter darkness.

As you entered the storm of your trial, people may have said that you just needed to "trust in the Lord." As you heard it again and again, it may have become more rote, like you agreed with it, but you did not hear it. I hate to say that Proverbs 3, particularly verses 5 and 6, have become more rote. They are great verses, but it has been overused to a point where it goes in one ear and out the other. Despite its overuse, God still speaks through these beautiful verses.

We were all created to know God, and you and I have a great privilege in knowing Christ personally. One of the struggles we have in this life, here on earth, is that we have never visibly seen

God. We see His creation and His work. We read His Word and pray to Him, but we have not seen Him at this point in time. We know He is here though! Part of our lives is realizing His role in every part, the big and the small, the meaningful and the mundane. We can see His hand is in every part of our lives.

In America, we assume we have earned everything. It is because of us we have so much. The refrigerator is full because we worked for the money to buy the food. We have shelter over our heads because of our hard work. We look at life and think it is because of us, but the truth is, that we need to acknowledge God in all things because each part of our lives was directly given or allowed by Him. God enabled you to work so your refrigerator is full and you have shelter over your head. God has allowed us to help each other out in times of need, so you have food and shelter. God is sovereign, and though sin presently reigns, He only allows it so that it can accomplish His purposes and give Him glory. It doesn't always make sense to our feeble and frail minds, but He is at work far beyond our understanding.

Acknowledging God's sovereignty over us is a way of moving toward spiritual healing. We have a place in Heaven just as God has a place when we understand who we are and what we are to do in Christ. When we acknowledge God's supremacy, all the pieces fit together, and the path ahead is straight, maybe not in reality, but certainly spiritually.

86

Best at Last

"Do not be anxious about anything, but in everything by prayer and supplication with thanksgiving let your requests be made known to God. And the peace of God, which surpasses all understanding, will guard your hearts and your minds in Christ Jesus."

~ **Philippians 4:6-7**

Calm and recovery look differently for each of us. For some, it will be a few days until recovery; for others like myself, the physical recovery takes a year or more, and yet for a few, there is no recovery this side of heaven. I have saved this entry as one of the last because it truly is the best in this book.

Patti Johnston and I became friends because of cancer and *Anchored in the Storm*. Her testimony and faith say so much about her desire to be completely and absolutely recovered before Jesus Christ. I will let Patti tell her story about seeing Jesus in the storm. I pray that you will see that even if the storm is over in our lives, we will never be fully recovered until we stand before Jesus Christ, His work fulfilled in us.

As I sit and contemplate my story, I am so truly humbled that Adam would ask me to be part of a book that could encourage or bless someone else going through similar circumstances. Looking back on my life, I can see how the Lord orchestrated everything so perfectly to bring me to this point in my battle with primary liver cancer.

I was raised in a Catholic home, went to 12 years of Catholic school, and always felt somewhat spiritual. I followed the rules and hoped one day I would be able to go to heaven when I died. I wanted to meet nice people that believed as I did. So, this is where the road to finding my Savior began.

I was now 21 and it was at that time I was introduced to a Baptist church with a very active young adult group. I felt at home, and soon I got very involved. It was there that I accepted Christ as my savior. I now understood it was a relationship not a religion. It was all so foreign to me, but I slowly continued my walk in my new found faith. I made mistakes, but the Lord was patient and full of grace.

Fast forward to January 2017 when my cancer journey began. It started with a fall, no other symptoms. Two days later I was in urgent care because of the severe pain I was having. What a shock when the doctor came back with the results of the CT scan and said I had a 15 cm tumor on my liver. My mind was thinking appendicitis. What was she saying?

On the way home my mind was going crazy. Thoughts and fears raced through me. What about leaving my husband, my kids and grandkids? I was not afraid to die but leaving them so soon, and the possibility of some of my grandkids never knowing me, or I them. The Lord calmed my fears and gave me ideas, like making memory books for them with lots of pictures of us together. That did ease some of my anxieties. So many times, I read Philippians 4:6-7 and thought, "What does that peace feel like or look like?" I have now experienced, firsthand, what that peace feels like. One of the greatest blessings I have received was that experience. I was told most people only live a year or so with primary liver cancer, but God in His perfect plan, has now blessed me with over 2 ½ years. He has a plan and knows the time. What a comfort that is to me.

Navigating through life is hard, especially when circumstances come your way that are life altering. Who better to trust than the one who made us and knows every hair on our head. Going through cancer, or any other trial, brings a new normal into our lives. Sometimes it settles in like a gentle rain, but sometimes it is like a big wave crashing over you that causes many other challenges.

Recently, I had another added challenge. I severely cut the bottom of my foot. So severely that it cut through muscle and many nerves. This certainly made everything harder. I couldn't walk, had many stitches, and a big swollen foot. I was almost completely dependent on my husband and others to do things for me. Again, humbling. Suffering does bring growth, but the road is tough at times. We grow through the crying, the pain, the down days and most of all the praying. Sometimes in my dark moments I wanted to hide away and not talk to anyone. But each day is a new day. God reminded me by infusing my days with blessings and provisions that were perfect for where I was at. Some days I just needed to get out of myself and see them.

Recovery is different for everyone as they journey through a trial. Mine was a continual recovery after every targeted chemo treatment and every procedure. Each one got harder for me mentally and physically, but it allowed me to see God at work, increase my faith and see how He was working in others around me. Our journeys are not just about us, but others in our scope of influence and most importantly, bringing glory to God. That is my hope, that my journey will encourage others to be drawn to Him.

I do not know how and when my journey will end, but I am confident that when the days God has ordained for me are up, I will be in the presence of the Lord, perfect and whole because of the sacrificial work Christ completed on the cross. Sometimes I cry out and say, "I want to be home with you," but I am reminded that in Psalms 46:10 it says, "Be Still and Know That I am God," and in Psalms 27:14, "Wait for the Lord; be strong and let your heart take courage; yes wait on the Lord."

No doubt, waiting is hard! What a comfort it is to me that God IS in control and uses all things and accomplishes His best for us in the throes of difficult times! Each detail of my journey is molding me into what God desires me to be. If I believe that God is who he shows Himself to be, and I do, then who am I to question what He allows in my life to draw me closer to Him and accomplish my spiritual growth? My faith has shown me that God is a God who can be trusted no matter what the circumstances.

A few weeks after writing the above passage, Patti received an update from her doctor and added the following to her story.

I just learned that my journey is coming to an end. I will not be receiving anymore treatment. The cancer is having its way in my body. My doctor spoke the word "hospice." You know sometime down the road your incurable cancer will take your life, but when you're sitting in a room and hear "hospice" and that you probably have six months or less to be on this earth, it stops you in your tracks. The fear of dying did not scare me, because I know my real home. My eternal home is truly at the end of this journey. What brought fear was the realization of what I was going to have to go through physically. I know how faithful the Lord has been throughout, so I take comfort in the fact that He will never leave me or forsake me, and He will see me through until the end.

All this is refining me and making me ready to be with my Lord. Take heart, lean on the one who will take you on a magnificent journey and love you with a love so great that you would had never experienced, except by having a personal relationship with Him. Our God is always good!!!

In December 2019, Patti stood in the presence of her Lord, passing from this world into His. Sin, pain, and cancer are no longer a part of her life; she is healed forevermore. She left an incredible legacy in the lives of her husband, Steve, her children, Kristen and Matt, their families, and the many friends whose lives are better because of her faith in Jesus Christ.

87

Hello, Hurricane

*"The Lord is my light and my salvation; whom shall I fear? The Lord
is the stronghold of my life; of whom shall I be afraid?"*

~ Psalm 27:1

"Hello, Hurricane" by Switchfoot

———◆———

So, here we are at the end of another *Anchored* book. I can't tell you what a joy it has been to come back, write another book, and sincerely and seriously pray for you. I pray for the readers of *Anchored in the Storm* each and every day, and it's a continuing joy to add you, reader of *Anchored to the Son*, to my prayers. Though I may never meet you in person, do know that I resolutely pray for you and want the Lord's absolute best for you.

As we part ways, I wanted to share another song with you, a song that best fits the end of our time and healing. While I pray for many years of peace and calm in your life, I have to quote what my pastor regularly reminds our congregation, "You're either coming out of a trial or you're going into a trial." So here we stand, parting ways into the calm. You may see a storm coming up quickly like a tornado in the Midwest, or maybe there is a hurricane forming in the Atlantic, but it is a bit offshore. Either way, a storm is coming, and I pray that after these two books, you are prepared for whatever may come.

"Hello, Hurricane" by Switchfoot is the last song I leave with you. When I hear this song, I think of this moment, the moment when the time of calm is over. Here we stand on the beach, the skies are getting cloudy, the temperature is dropping, there is a growing wind, and a storm is brewing. Before we part, there is one last song I want to share with you that best fits this time of transition from calm to storm to calm to storm, on and on until we go to be with the Lord. There is a storm on the horizon, a storm is coming, a trial is coming. I hate to say that, but my pastor is right; one is coming, and it could be a small storm, or it could be a whopper! We know a storm is coming, so let us best prepare.

The first lines of the song as you stand under a clouding sky:

I've been watching the skies

They've been turning blood red

Not a doubt in my mind anymore

There's a storm up ahead

When I think of those words, I think of old men sitting on an old porch talking about how their ailments predict the weather. It is comical to consider it, but we can feel a storm is coming. What do we do with that information? How are we going to prepare? How are we going to handle the reddening and darkening skies?

Hello hurricane

You're not enough

Hello hurricane

You can't silence my love

I've got doors and windows boarded up

All your dead end fury is not enough

You can't silence my love

The calm has a way of softening life, making us more complacent, easier to forget that we went through a trial. Having lived in California my entire life, I am supposed to be prepared for the "Big One," the earthquake that will forever change the state. Many of us, including myself, are not the best prepared, though we know one is coming, whether big or not. In our walks with the Lord as Christ-followers we are to be prepared for what the Lord has in store, for each day of our lives, to share the gospel with whomever we encounter; we are to be prepared.

Paul writes to his mentee, Timothy, in 2 Timothy 4:1-2, "I charge you in the presence of God and of Christ Jesus, who is to judge the living and the dead, and by his appearing and his kingdom: preach the word, be ready in season and out of season; reprove, rebuke, and exhort, with complete patience and teaching." Paul reminds us of our position in Christ, that God must be our priority in all circumstances. We are to be ready to live the gospel, to share the gospel, to trust in Him who wrote the gospel, and Him who died so that we may be in Christ.

Everything I have I count as loss

Everything I have is stripped away

Before I started building

I counted up these costs

There's nothing left for you to take away

So, at the end of the calm and the start of the storm, what are you holding to? What of the old life has creeped back? At the end of this, do you count all as loss compared to the glorious relationship you have in Christ? These are questions we need to dwell on in all parts of life.

You and I stand prepared for the storm, but also prepared for the calm. I pray the Lord's presence and hand of grace upon you!

Father,

Here we are once again, laying our lives in the calm and in the storm at Your feet. We have experienced such tragic storms and such precious calms, all directed by Your sovereign hand for Your glory and Your kingdom. We may not always understand the workings of Your hand in our lives, but we know and trust that they always work out for Your good purposes. You say in Romans 8:28, "And we know that for those that love God all things work together for good, for those who are called according to his purpose." Father, you have called us according to Your purpose, a life in you. In that life, You orchestrate all parts, and whatever storms are coming, we trust that You will be by our side, present the entire time, taking the burden of the storm more than we do.

I lift up to You each reader of this book, and pray that Your hand will lead and guide them on the paths of life, from the narrow mountain paths to the wide roads to the horizon. I pray for each reader. Your unique call on each of us has brought us all together, and I pray for those we may all encounter on this journey of life. The world in which we live is so broken, so lost, and though our hearts are eager for a place in Your presence in Heaven, we each know that we have a job, a purpose, and a duty here that has yet to be completely fulfilled. Help us each to take our role in this world seriously, laying aside all those things that tie us down to the world, laying them at Your feet that we might take on the tasks you have for us ahead in this life, unburdened by the constraints of life on this earth. We pray Lord that you would be honored and glorified by our work for Your kingdom and help when we need reminders of who we are in You.

To You be the Glory O, Lord! Amen.

Acknowledgements

"For it is all for your sake, so that as grace extends to more and more people it may increase thanksgiving, to the glory of God."

~ **2 Corinthians 4:15**

———◆———

No matter who we are, no one life can be lived alone, at least lived well alone. When I was diagnosed with cancer, I saw many come alongside me and my family, in prayer and presence. They lived life with us throughout those dark days. As the storm calmed, so many naturally returned to their normal life, as I started my "new normal" life. Friendships were renewed, strengthened, and many new friendships were created, all cherished very much.

When it came to writing a book there were a few people who stepped up to embrace what God had done during the calm that many may know and pursue Christ through this book. Each one played a part of sharing their talents, their encouragement, and their vision to see the Lord work once again through the written word.

To Jesus—Once again, I found myself in a place and a journey I never imagined for my life. While I thought the calm would come smoothly, it hasn't always, but like the theme of our relationship, you have demonstrated a faithfulness beyond my understanding. As with the storm, you have walked with me each step into the calm. In many respects the future out of cancer is uncertain, but like your faithfulness throughout my life, I know Your faithfulness will continue again until we meet face to face, and in that first moment to the end of eternity!

To Mom and Dad—The storm took it out on each of us in different ways, but for the last 38 years we have taken life together and the calm was no different than the storm in this life, though certainly less moment by moment living. Like I said in *Anchored in the Storm*, "Thank you" can hardly express the gratitude and love I have for you two (and the girls too!). Love you guys!!!

To Crossroads Community Church—As the past five years have changed my life, so has Crossroads changed over these five years, not because of me, but because of God's work through our pastors, staff, and people. Our days ahead are all His and as we have storms and calms ahead, I know God is going to work in ways beyond our imagining. The Lord be with us all as we seek to trust Him, live His Word, and share the plan for salvation with a world in a storm all its own.

And a special thank you to the brothers and sisters in my small group, men's Bible study, and who serve in ministry. You have prayed for this book just as much as I have. Thank you!

To Todd and Stacey Smith—These past five years have been extraordinary and the Lord has once again worked in each of our lives and those of Crossroads to amaze us. Thank you for once again bringing your great wisdom and insight to the pages of this book. Your work in my life and the life of the church is an incredible blessing to us all and even more so to the Lord! It's been an absolute joy to walk this 14-year journey of Crossroads with you both!

To R.W. and Beth Mackey—As the years have passed in this life, from being a kid at church with your own kids, to being a student under your leadership at The Master's College, to serving alongside you at Crossroads Community Church, you have quietly and wisely displayed an incredible faith in Christ and inspired me in my own relationship with Christ. Your own trials once again inspired my own faith in the Lord. You both have been an absolute blessing to my life!

To Patti Johnston—My dear friend, it was cancer and *Anchored in the Storm* that brought us together and though our friendship had not been long, I cannot tell you how much I have learned from you and your beautiful example of laying your life down at the feet of Christ, knowing each and every part of this life is orchestrated by His precious hands. You are the one person I have met in all these years that completely understands my long desire to be in heaven with Christ. You are now home with Christ and experiencing joys beyond any this world could ever have.

To Mark Gooby—The first cover you created blew my mind and you astounded me once again with another beautiful cover. Your ability to take what is in my mind and put it onto a cover amazes me. When I think of both books, the first thing that comes to mind is your cover art. God has given you a great talent that blesses Crossroads each week and am blessed by your work on these books, and maybe more in the future. Thank you, Mark!

To Jenni O'Shea—You stepped in to embrace the editing work when life was at its craziest, but you knew God was working and as I have learned over the years, you have a beautiful perspective on what God is doing. I could not have asked for a more beautiful critique of what the Lord laid upon my heart. Thank you for clarifying, honing, and refining areas that needed your perfect touch. It was a pleasure having you join the "*Anchored*" team! And still can't believe how God has blessed your wonderful family! Such a joy to pray all these years and see perfection in God's answers!

To John Manning—We have yet to meet in person, but am so grateful for you formatting the book and making it a masterpiece to read. Thank you for your help in something that was quite frustrating for me to do. You answered a prayer and stepped up to the plate to complete this book. Thank you!

To the Quiet Warriors—You and I both have made it out of the storm into a "new normal" of life. As I pray daily for the readers of *Anchored in the Storm*, so I pray for you, the readers of Anchored to the Son. We have had the incredible privilege of God working both quietly and mightily in our lives. It is an absolute joy to walk this life with you, even if we do not meet this side of Heaven. You are much loved and prayed for. I leave you, dear reader, with this quote from the great missionary, William Carey, "Expect great things from God, attempt great things for God."

Made in the USA
Las Vegas, NV
04 May 2021

22483218R00182